Map Key

(continued)

Map Key *(continued)*

West Side of RMNP

NORTHWEST SIDE OF ROCKY MOUNTAIN NATIONAL PARK
(Trail Ridge Road, Colorado River Headwaters Area, and Never Summer Range)

SOUTHWEST SIDE OF ROCKY MOUNTAIN NATIONAL PARK
(Tonahutu Area, East Inlet Area, and North Inlet Area)

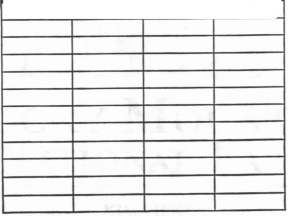

R AIN

Day & Overnight Hikes: Rocky Mountain National Park

Copyright © 2016 by Kim Lipker
All rights reserved
Published by Menasha Ridge Press
Distributed by Publishers Group West
Printed in the United States of America
Second edition, first printing

Text and cover design: Ian Szymkowiak/Palace Press International with updates by Annie Long
Cover and interior photographs: Kim Lipker
Cartography and elevation profiles: Kim Lipker and Steve Jones
Indexer: Rich Carlson

Library of Congress Cataloging-in-Publication Data
Names: Lipker, Kim, 1969-
Title: Day & overnight hikes, Rocky Mountain National Park / Kim Lipker.
Description: 2nd Edition. | Birmingham, Alabama : Menasha Ridge Press, [2016] |
"Distributed by Publishers Group West"—T.p. verso. | Includes index.
Identifiers: LCCN 2015043786| ISBN 9781634040167 | ISBN 9781634040174 (Ebook)
Subjects: LCSH: Hiking—Colorado—Rocky Mountain National Park—Guidebooks. |
   National parks and reserves—Colorado—Guidebooks. |
   Rocky Mountain National Park (Colo.)—Guidebooks.
Classification: LCC GV199.42.C2 L57 2016 | DDC 796.5109788/69—dc23
LC record available at lccn.loc.gov/2015043786

 Menasha Ridge Press
   2204 First Ave. S., Suite 102
   Birmingham, Alabama 35233
   menasharidge.com

DISCLAIMER

This book is meant only as a guide to select trails in the vicinity of Rocky Mountain National Park and does not guarantee hiker safety in any way—you hike at your own risk. Neither Menasha Ridge Press nor Kim Lipker is liable for property loss or damage, personal injury, or death that result in any way from accessing or hiking the trails described in the following pages. Please be aware that hikers have been injured in the Rocky Mountain National Park area. Be especially cautious when walking on or near boulders, steep inclines, and drop-offs, and do not attempt to explore terrain that may be beyond your abilities. Please read the introduction to this book carefully and consider getting additional safety information and guidance from other sources. Familiarize yourself thoroughly with the areas you intend to visit before venturing out. Ask questions, and prepare for the unforeseen. Familiarize yourself with current weather reports, maps of the area you intend to visit, and any relevant park regulations.

TABLE OF CONTENTS

East Side of Rocky Mountain National Park

NORTHEAST SIDE OF ROCKY MOUNTAIN NATIONAL PARK
(North Fork Area and Mummy Range)   27

EAST CENTER OF ROCKY MOUNTAIN NATIONAL PARK
(Gorge Lakes Area and Bear Lake Area)   45

SOUTHEAST SIDE OF ROCKY MOUNTAIN NATIONAL PARK
(Longs Peak Area and Wild Basin Area) 95

West Side of Rocky Mountain National Park

NORTHWEST SIDE OF ROCKY MOUNTAIN NATIONAL PARK
*(Trail Ridge Road, Colorado River Headwaters Area, and
Never Summer Range)* 133

SOUTHWEST SIDE OF ROCKY MOUNTAIN NATIONAL PARK
(Tonahutu Area, East Inlet Area, and North Inlet Area) 157

ACKNOWLEDGMENTS

THANK YOU TIMES INFINITY to those folks who helped with the first edition of this guide—they helped form the backbone of this book: Abby Balfany; Bruce Becker; Michael Bollinger; Christa Gorman; Russell Helms; Lindsay Hopper; Jen Janssen; Kelly Josephs; Anna, Alex, and Emma Lipker; Ruth and Roger Lipker (Mom and Dad); Molly Merkle; Johnny Molloy; Robert Muchow (Grandpa); MaryAnn Muchow; Paul Muchow; Tricia Parks; Anne Perkins; Lindsay Smith and Paul Chavez; Diane Stanko and Marty Martinez; Nancy Stilson-Herzog; Murielle Watzky-Brewer; and John and Fiona Wilson.

For the second edition, I must also thank all of the first responders and volunteers involved in the 2013 flood-recovery efforts. Thank you to friends and family who support me in everything that I do: Leslie Ballentine, Kris Baltrum, Tommi Sue Cox, Holly Cross, Bob and Carole Fixter, Tim Jackson, Steve Jones, Suellen May, Shannon McConathy, Lynda Moore, Lisa Olson, Renee Putman, Todd Sledge, Julie Stajduhar, and Tanya Sylvan.

 DEDICATION

FOR KAREN LIPKER, my favorite little sister. We'll always have good memories of Estes Park and the infamous "What does 'No Vacancy' mean?" family trip.

AND FOR MARYANN MUCHOW. I miss you!

Author and her sister in Rocky Mountain National Park circa 1970s on the old National Park Railway train

PREFACE TO THE SECOND EDITION

IN YOUR HANDS is the newest edition of *Day & Overnight Hikes: Rocky Mountain National Park.* The first edition was published in 2008, and 2015 marked Rocky Mountain National Park's 100th anniversary! That's right: A celebration of 100 years of stewardship and protection of one of our nation's most beloved national parks. This edition, published with centennial pride, includes flood-impact updates, revised maps, an expanded Longs Peak profile, and a new hike.

Coming back to revise this book was rough. In 2013, a flood devastated the east side of Rocky Mountain National Park and her neighboring communities. More than 18 inches of rain fell in three days in September. Damage to the park was minor in comparison to the disastrous flooding downstream that affected 14 counties, a dozen towns, and six major rivers in Colorado. Rocky Mountain National Park contains many of the headwaters of the 2013 flood, and the park received significant damage on bridges, roads, and trails. Two years after the flood, a fresh visit and a new eye are warranted, and all updates are reflected in this book.

This was also the year that I found out my aunt MaryAnn had lung cancer. Six weeks after her diagnosis, she died. Her memorial was a few weeks before the floods. She was a longtime resident of Estes Park and was one of the many reasons I visited the area so often. This was a hard book to revisit with her gone. She worked at the iconic Stanley Hotel for more than 22 years. A few days before she died, MaryAnn presented her "community family" of colleagues a Stanley Hotel commemorative quilt that she spent two years designing and sewing. The quilt has been mounted and is now on display at the hotel. When you visit the area, be sure to stop in and see it.

Flood!

THE SEPTEMBER 2013 FLOOD was unexpected. It stirred memories of two other major floods that are still on the minds and in the hearts of those affected. Mother Nature can turn tiny streams into walls of water, mud, and debris. Human error also can push the limits of nature. The Big Thompson flood in 1976 was a natural disaster, and the 1982 Lawn Lake flood was the failure of a dam constructed in 1903. Both floods were tragic in terms of loss; however, both provided a study of recovery.

Most of Rocky Mountain National Park is designated wilderness area where self-reliance is expected. Due to the 2013 flood, park visitors may encounter conditions that they have never experienced. Driving up either canyon to the park from Lyons or Longmont on the east side of the Continental Divide is a testament. Homes still hang in the balance, waiting for repair, and eerie signs of damage still mark the way.

In the park, visitors may find missing bridges, missing trail, uneven trail, unstable slopes, fallen trees, and rutted steps. Some water crossings may be difficult, and some directional trail signs also may be missing. The park has worked on short trail detours and is in the process of constructing longer, more sustainable trails. They have worked tirelessly to identify the best ways to protect cultural resources and preserve wilderness character. All trails and backcountry camping sites featured in this book are currently open to the public, but portions of the trails may be badly damaged.

The park has done a fabulous job of keeping visitors informed. Be diligent about checking current conditions. Pay attention to all warning signs posted throughout the park. Special signs tell visitors to watch for damaged or missing footbridges, high water at stream crossings, missing and damaged trail tread, rough trail surfaces, damaged or missing water bars and steps, deep ruts making travel difficult, unstable steep slopes, rock fall and falling trees, standing water on trails, and missing directional signs. The disclaimer is always there that states: Travel at your own risk. Safety is your responsibility.

Special warnings where bridges are still missing on trails say that some river crossings are not recommended. Hazards include cold, fast-moving water; slippery rocks and logs; and risk of injury of drowning.

PREFACE TO THE FIRST EDITION

ROCKY MOUNTAIN NATIONAL PARK

THE CROWNING JEWEL of anyone's hiking or backpacking history is Rocky Mountain National Park. That's why it is such an honor for me to write a book about an extraordinary national park that is right in my backyard. If you are lucky enough to live within driving distance of Rocky Mountain National Park, you know what I mean, and you'll also find that the 31 hikes featured here may keep you busy for years to come.

Visitors to Colorado will most likely join thousands of others who make their way to Rocky Mountain National Park every year (3.4 million, to be exact). It is truly an experience not to be missed. More than 110 mountain peaks tower over the 415 square miles of hiking trails, picnic spots, waterfalls, cold lakes, and bountiful wildlife.

It was my job to narrow the aforementioned hiking trails and 269 backcountry campsites into useful recommendations for day hikes and overnight hikes in Rocky Mountain National Park. The selections were made based on a variety of criteria and are what make up this manageable and well-rounded guidebook.

Rocky Mountain National Park is located northwest of Denver, spanning Grand and Larimer counties and bordered on the west by the town of Grand Lake and on the east by the town of Estes Park. The park is revered by residents on Colorado's Western Slope and the Front Range. This is especially true of all of those that can see the towering peaks from their car windows when they drive around the northern part of the Colorado Front Range (Fort Collins to Boulder to Denver).

Adjacent to Indian Peaks Wilderness and Comanche Peaks Wilderness to the north, and to Never Summer Wilderness to the west, the park is also surrounded by Routt, Roosevelt, and Arapaho National Forests. Now is an exciting time for Rocky Mountain National Park because it's progressing toward wilderness designation, for which it has been a candidate since the Wilderness Act was passed in 1964. The park was established by Congress in 1915 with the help of naturalist Enos Mills and F. O. Stanley. In 1974 President Nixon

A young hiker takes a short rest to appreciate the beauty of nature. Rocky Mountain National Park in the summer is breathtaking and warm. Never too hot, maybe a little crowded, but the whole park is awash in color.

recommended 239,835 acres for wilderness designation, providing permanent protection for the park. The area has been managed as wilderness since the 1960s, its wilderness qualities protected and celebrated by several generations of park employees and park visitors.

The elevations in Rocky Mountain National Park range from 7,500 feet to 14,255 feet, encompassing green valleys and alpine tundra. Longs Peak is the highest peak, and Mount Meeker, at 13,911 feet, rises to the south. Seventy-two mountains exceed 12,000 feet, and more than 110 of the peaks soar above 10,000 feet. (That's almost 2 miles above sea level!) The valleys below these high peaks are thick with forests of lodgepole pine, juniper, and spruce, and rich with wildlife.

Rocky Mountain National Park is home to 150 lakes and plenty of rivers, streams, and waterfalls. The Colorado River marks its birthplace in the park. The Continental Divide runs northwest to southeast through the park. Snowmelt and rainwater to the west of the Great Divide flows toward the Pacific Ocean; runoff to the east is bound for the Gulf of Mexico and the Atlantic Ocean.

People are also a part of the Rocky Mountain National Park wilderness. Hikers, anglers, miners, homesteaders, pioneers, Native Americans, and more have made a mark on the park's history.

During the research for this book, I became nostalgic for all the years I have spent in the park. My grandma, grandpa, aunt, cousin, and another aunt and uncle all live or have lived here. I've even lived in Estes Park. My cousin was married at the historic Stanley Hotel during the writing of this book. My grandpa also passed away during my last days of research, 10 years to the month after my grandma died.

It was a joy to hike with my sister and recall the fun we've had in the park—from her falling into the ashes of an old campfire (in the olden days, of course) to hearing about Grandma's high school senior trip to Longs Peak (in the very olden days—the 1930s to be exact). In a way, the mountains are tied to Grandma, and not a day goes by that I don't think of her.

My respect for the management of the park has never waned. The trails here are constantly upgraded, as are the facilities in and outside the park. I recommend visiting the area in the fall, when the elk are in the valleys for their bugling (mating) season. Crowds are thinning, the colors are changing, and the weather is still quite pleasant.

Lesser-known hikes, such as the hikes on the west side of the park, were nice to revisit. These hikes tend to be longer and less crowded and are great for travelers spending a night or two around the Grand Lake area. Onahu Creek Trailhead: Onahu Creek Trail and Green Mountain Trail Loop is a perfect example. The other hikes in the southwest side of Rocky Mountain National Park are located in the Tonahutu, East Inlet, and North Inlet areas. These are hikes that border Grand Lake and travel through the other side of the park.

The best way to explore the history of Rocky Mountain National Park and the surrounding area is to visualize those people who have walked the trails before you. Pioneers who just crossed over the Continental Divide and claimed their homestead can be revisited on trails such as the Holzwarth Historic Site: Never Summer Ranch. Other hikes on the northwest side of Rocky Mountain National Park encompass the areas around Trail Ridge Road, Colorado River Headwaters, and the Never Summer Range. These trails range from flat meadow hikes to alpine tundra treks.

On the east side, you'll find some nice surprises among the old tried-and-true. An overall favorite hike of mine is Cow Creek Trailhead: Bridal Veil Falls. Other great hikes on the northeast side of Rocky Mountain National Park are in the North Fork Area and the Mummy Range. However, two people did get lost on the trail to the Cache Campsite while I was writing this book. Be sure to take the book along if you go.

The East Center of Rocky Mountain National Park, where you'll find Gorge Lakes and Bear Lake, is the most crowded area of the park. If possible, try to hike here on weekdays in the spring, fall, or winter. All of the hikes in this region are unique in terrain and difficulty, thus their popularity.

On the southeast side of Rocky Mountain National Park is where you'll find the infamous Longs Peak, along with the Wild Basin area. Be sure to try out lesser-known hikes here, such as Sandbeach Lake, another personal favorite.

If you tour Estes Park, be sure to stop at the Stanley Hotel. My aunt was a waitress there for more than 20 years, and the hotel is rich with stories—they say that Stephen King found the inspiration for *The Shining* while staying here.

In the time that it took me to research and write this book, many people were lost and found while hiking in Rocky Mountain National Park. That serves as a reminder to please be careful on the trail and always hike with a buddy. At the very least, let someone know where you're going and when you expect to be back.

Thank you for buying or borrowing this book. Be assured that I had you, the reader, in mind during every one of my hikes. By picking up this book, you should also be willing to become a steward of the wilderness and pledge to preserve our national parks. I want my children and future generations to be able to experience the joy of Rocky Mountain National Park.

Recommended Hikes

RECOMMENDED HIKES

RECOMMENDED HIKES

INTRODUCTION

How to Use This Guidebook

The Overview Map and Overview Map Key

USE THE OVERVIEW MAP on the inside front cover to assess the exact locations of each hike's primary trailhead. Each hike's number appears on the overview map, on the map key facing the overview map, in the table of contents, and at the top of each hike profile.

The book is organized by region, as indicated in the table of contents. The hikes within each region are noted as day hikes or overnight hikes in the map key and in the table of contents.

Trail Maps

Each hike contains a detailed map showing the trailhead, route, significant features, facilities, and topographic landmarks such as creeks, overlooks, and peaks. The author gathered map data by carrying a GPS unit while hiking, then sent that data to Menasha Ridge Press's expert cartographers. Each trailhead's GPS coordinates are included with each profile (see next page).

Elevation Profiles

Corresponding to the trail map, each hike contains a detailed elevation profile that provides a quick look at the trail from the side, enabling you to visualize how the trail rises and falls. Key points along the way are labeled. Note the number of feet between each tick mark on the vertical axis (the height scale). To avoid making flat hikes look steep and steep hikes appear flat, height scales are used throughout the book to provide an accurate image of the hike's difficulty.

OPPOSITE *Hike 8 The Loch* (see page 58). Alberta Falls on The Loch Trail is easy to access and a magnificent reward.

GPS Trailhead Coordinates

In addition to highly specific trail outlines, this book also includes the latitude (north) and longitude (west) coordinates for each trailhead. The latitude–longitude grid system is likely quite familiar to you, but here's a refresher, pertinent to visualizing the coordinates.

Imaginary lines of latitude—called parallels and approximately 69 miles apart from each other—run horizontally around the globe. Each parallel is indicated by degrees from the equator (established to be 0°): up to 90°N at the North Pole and down to 90°S at the South Pole.

Imaginary lines of longitude—called meridians—run perpendicular to lines of latitude and are likewise indicated by degrees. Starting from 0° at the Prime Meridian in Greenwich, England, they continue to the east and west until they meet 180° later at the International Date Line in the Pacific Ocean. At the equator, longitude lines also are approximately 69 miles apart, but that distance narrows as the meridians converge toward the North and South Poles.

In this book, latitude and longitude are expressed in degree–decimal minute format. For example, the coordinates for Hike 1, Cow Creek Trailhead: Bridal Veil Falls (page 28) are as follows: N40°25.743' W105°29.998'. For more on GPS technology, visit **usgs.gov.**

The Hike Profile

In addition to maps, each hike contains a concise but informative narrative of the hike from beginning to end. This descriptive text is enhanced with at-a-glance ratings and information, GPS-based trailhead coordinates, and accurate driving directions that lead you from a major road to the parking area that is most convenient to the trailhead.

At the top of the section for each hike is a box that provides the hiker pertinent information: quality of scenery, appropriateness for children, difficulty of hike, quality of solitude expected, condition of trail, flood impact, hike distance, approximate hiking time, and outstanding highlights of the trip. The first five categories are rated using a five-star system, with five indicating the most scenic, child-friendly, difficult, and solitary hikes and the most pristine trail condition.

Flood-impact ratings are listed in conjunction with the trail condition. A one-star or two-star rating means that flooding did impact the trail but damage is minimal, a three-star rating signifies more severe flood impact, and a five-star rating means that the trail is closed due to the flood. We have not included any five-star flood-impact hikes in this book. There are, however, four-star flood-impact ratings, and those hikes should be approached with caution and respect. All other ratings may fluctuate due to the flood-impact rating. For example, a flood-impact rating of two is probably okay for children; a rating of four may not be.

Hiking times are estimated based on an average hiking speed of 2 to 3 miles per hour, with time built in for pauses at overlooks and brief rests. Overnight hiking times account for the effort of carrying a backpack.

Following each box is a brief, italicized description of the hike. A more detailed account follows in which trail junctions, stream crossings, and trailside features are noted along with their distance from the trailhead. Flip through the book, read the descriptions, and choose a hike that appeals to you.

Weather

ROCKY MOUNTAIN NATIONAL PARK WEATHER is always changing. Temperatures drop, and precipitation increases proportionate to the altitude. The higher the elevation, the lower the temperature. Be prepared and dress in layers. Always prepare for chilly conditions. Remember: you can remove a layer you're wearing, but you can't put on a layer you didn't bring. On the next page is detailed information about the area's weather.

SUMMER *(June, July, August)*
Expect sunny mornings and afternoon thunderstorms accompanied by lightning. Nights are clear and cool.

FALL *(September, October, November)*
Expect mornings with frost, pleasant and clear afternoons, and chilly nights. There is a possibility of early snowstorms.

WINTER *(December, January, February, March)*

Expect cool to very cold mornings, high winds, blizzard conditions, and large temperature fluctuations.

Temperature and Precipitation *(Temperatures shown are averages.)*

ESTES PARK (ELEVATION 7,522')				
MONTH	**HIGH**	**LOW**	**PRECIPITATION**	**SNOW**
JANUARY	39 F°	16 F°	0.37"	4.6"
FEBRUARY	41 F°	17 F°	0.45"	6.3"
MARCH	45 F°	21 F°	0.86"	7.8"
APRIL	53 F°	27 F°	1.28"	3.8"
MAY	62 F°	34 F°	2.02"	0.5"
JUNE	73 F°	41 F°	1.76"	0.1"
JULY	78 F°	46 F°	2.21"	0.0"
AUGUST	77 F°	45 F°	1.86"	0.0"
SEPTEMBER	70 F°	38 F°	1.17"	0.5"
OCTOBER	60 F°	30 F°	0.81"	1.0"
NOVEMBER	46 F°	23 F°	0.60"	3.8"
DECEMBER	40 F°	18 F°	0.47"	5.7"
GRAND LAKE (ELEVATION 8,369')				
MONTH	**HIGH**	**LOW**	**PRECIPITATION**	**SNOW**
JANUARY	31 F°	2 F°	1.68"	29.6"
FEBRUARY	35 F°	4 F°	1.43"	22.5"
MARCH	40 F°	10 F°	1.54"	19.5"
APRIL	49 F°	19 F°	1.88"	16.8"
MAY	59 F°	27 F°	1.94"	4.7"
JUNE	70 F°	33 F°	1.60"	0.4"
JULY	75 F°	37 F°	2.06"	0.0"
AUGUST	74 F°	36 F°	2.08"	0.0"
SEPTEMBER	67 F°	29 F°	1.64"	1.1"
OCTOBER	57 F°	22 F°	1.28"	5.9"
NOVEMBER	40 F°	12 F°	1.33"	18.9"
DECEMBER	32 F°	3 F°	1.66"	27.5"

SPRING *(April, May)*

Temperatures are unpredictable at best; expect deep, wet snowfalls.

All seasons get a healthy helping of Colorado sunshine.

Altitude Sickness

Nothing ruins an outing more often than the body's resistance to altitude adjustment. The illness is usually characterized by vomiting, shortness of breath, extreme headache, light-headedness, sleeplessness, and an overall sick feeling. Our advice: take it easy. When traveling to a higher altitude, give your body a day or two to adjust to less oxygen, hotter sun, and less air pressure. Drink plenty of water, and avoid alcohol and cigarettes. Wear sunglasses and sunscreen. Yes, sometimes avoiding illness is that easy. (However, if serious symptoms persist, locate the nearest emergency room or call 911.)

Lightning

Get an early start on all hikes that go above treeline. Violent storms are common in June, July, and August. Try to reach high-altitude summits by 1 p.m. and turn back when the weather turns bad. If you get caught in a lightning storm above treeline, stay off ridgetops, spread out if you are in a group, and squat or sit on a foam pad with your feet together. Keep away from rock outcroppings and isolated trees. If someone has been struck by lightning, be prepared to use CPR to help restore breathing and heartbeat.

Hypothermia

Hypothermia occurs when your core body temperature is dangerously low. This condition can occur at any time of the year, and cold temperatures, wind, and rain and snow set the stage for complications. Look for signs of shivering, loss of coordination, and loss of judgment. Prevention in the form of preparation is your best defense against getting cold to the core. Remember the mantra "wet is not warm" to prevent hypothermia. Keep your inside layer as dry as possible.

CORSAR

The Colorado Outdoor Recreation Search and Rescue Card (CORSAR) can be purchased at more than 300 retailers in the state or online at **dola.colorado .gov/sar.** You can buy a one-year card for $3, or spend $12 and buy a five-year card. CORSAR is not insurance—it does not pay for medical transportation, which may include helicopter flights or ground ambulance. The card does allow reimbursement to county sheriffs for costs included on a mission.

These expenses can include mileage, meals, equipment, gasoline, and rental fees (horses, ATVs, aircraft) for vehicles used in the search. It says right on the CORSAR website that "you have helped ensure that trained and well-equipped search and rescue teams will respond should you become lost or in need of rescue and they will not have to incur undue expense due to your emergency."

Avalanches

When in snow-packed backcountry, avoid steep slopes and gullies where avalanches occur. Open slopes of 30 to 45 degrees can be loaded with dangerous masses of snow, easily triggered by the presence of one or more travelers. Check at the visitor centers for current snow conditions.

Sun

Ultraviolet light is strong in the mountains because there is less atmosphere for sunlight to pass through. Wear sunscreen, a hat, and sunglasses, and consider wearing long sleeves and pants. Sunburn can creep up on the most unsuspecting hikers, whether it's sunny, cloudy, hot, or cold.

Swift Water

Mountain streams can be dangerous during high snow runoff in May and June. Even a narrow stream may be deep and fast, as well as cold. Remain back from the banks of streams and rivers, especially if you cannot see the bottom. Provide proper supervision for children who tend to be attracted to water. Rocks at the streamside and in the stream are often slippery, and water beneath them may be deep. Powerful currents in park streams can pull a person under water and pin him or her below the surface. In case of a flash flood, climb to safety.

HIKE 30 *Tonahutu Creek Trail to Renegade Campsite to Flattop Mountain (see page 168). Elk are plentiful in Rocky Mountain National Park, and this beautiful cow was spotted on Big Horn Flats on the way to the Renegade Campsite.*

Water

HOW MUCH IS ENOUGH? Well, one simple physiological fact should convince you to err on the side of excess when deciding how much water to pack: A hiker working hard in 90°F heat needs about 10 quarts of fluid per day. That's 2.5 gallons—12 large water bottles or 16 small ones. So pack one or two bottles even for short hikes.

Some hikers and backpackers hit the trail prepared to purify water found along the route. This method, while less dangerous than drinking it untreated, comes with risks. Purifiers with ceramic filters are the safest. Many hikers pack along the slightly distasteful tetraglycine–hydroperiodide tablets to debug water (sold under the names Potable Aqua, Coughlan's, and others).

Probably the most common waterborne "bug" that hikers face is giardia, which may not hit until one to four weeks after ingestion. It will have you living in the bathroom, passing noxious rotten-egg gas, vomiting, and shivering with chills. Other parasites to worry about include E. coli and cryptosporidium, both of which are harder to kill than giardia.

For most people, the pleasures of hiking make carrying water a relatively minor price to pay to remain healthy. If you're tempted to drink found water, do so only if you understand the risks involved. Better yet, hydrate prior to your hike, carry (and drink) 6 ounces of water for every mile you plan to hike, and hydrate after the hike.

The Ten Essentials

SEE APPENDIX A: Camping Equipment Checklist (page 179) for a comprehensive summer backpacking gear checklist.

One of the first rules of hiking is to be prepared for anything. The simplest way to be prepared is to carry the "Ten Essentials." In addition to carrying the items listed below, you need to know how to use them, especially navigation items. Always consider worst-case scenarios like getting lost, hiking back in the dark, broken gear (for example, a broken hip strap on your pack or a water filter getting plugged), twisting an ankle, or a brutal thunderstorm. The items listed below don't cost a lot of money, don't take up much room in a pack, and don't weigh much, but they might just save your life.

WATER: durable bottles, and water treatment such as iodine or a filter

MAP: preferably a topo map and a trail map with a route description

COMPASS: a high-quality compass

FIRST-AID KIT: a good-quality kit, including first-aid instructions

KNIFE: a multitool device with pliers is best

LIGHT: flashlight or headlamp with extra bulbs and batteries

FIRE: windproof matches or lighter and fire starter

EXTRA FOOD: you should always have food in your pack when you've finished hiking

EXTRA CLOTHES: rain protection, warm layers, gloves, warm hat

SUN PROTECTION: sunglasses, lip balm, sunblock, sun hat

First-Aid Kit

A TYPICAL FIRST-AID KIT may contain more items than you might think necessary. The ones in the list that follows are just the basics. Pre-packaged kits in waterproof bags (Atwater Carey and Adventure Medical make a variety of kits) are available. Even though quite a few items are listed below, they pack down into a small space:

- Ace bandages or Spenco joint wraps
- Antibiotic ointment *(Neosporin or the generic equivalent)*
- Acetaminophen or ibuprofen
- Band-Aids
- Benadryl or the generic equivalent, diphenhydramine *(in case of allergic reactions)*
- Butterfly-closure bandages
- Epinephrine in a prefilled syringe *(for severe allergic reactions to such things as bee stings; usually only available by prescription)*
- Gauze *(one roll)*
- Gauze compress pads *(a half dozen 4x4-inch pads)*
- Hydrogen peroxide or iodine
- Insect repellent

- Matches or pocket lighter
- Moleskin or Spenco "Second Skin"
- Sunscreen
- Whistle *(it's more effective in signaling rescuers than your voice)*

THE FOLLOWING ITEMS are optional but worth their weight:

- Aluminum foil
- Carabiners
- Dark chocolate *(at least 60% cocoa)*
- Disinfectant wipes *(baby wipes work, too)*
- Foam pad *(for lightning strikes)*
- GPS receiver
- High-energy food and drinks
- Snakebite kit
- Watch

- Bandana
- Cellular phone *(emergencies only)*
- Digital camera
- Extra batteries
- Garbage bag
- Hand warmers *(air activated)*
- Plastic bags with zip closure
- Toilet paper

Kim's Tips for Hiking and Camping with Children

BRINGING YOUR KIDS to Rocky Mountain National Park can be a great way to introduce the young to nature. It's also wonderful exercise and an even better family-bonding experience. It's time away from laundry, cell phones, and dishes—just you and the kids and nature.

Planning and Pacing

It's not advisable to take newborns out in the wild, but short walks in a stroller or a baby carrier are wonderful sensory and bonding opportunities. When my babies cried, I'd walk around our yard and point out leaves, trees, flowers, and birds. It calmed them and was a great way to build up to longer jaunts.

HIKE 8 *The Loch (see page 58). Hiking in Rocky Mountain National Park is very family-friendly, and there are hikes for every age and ability. These two young hikers are enjoying a trek on the trail to the Loch.*

HIKE 28 *Lake Verna Campsite (see page 158). From your tent at the Lake Verna Campsite, you will see this: alpine peaks and Lake Verna. Where else can you get a view like this?*

For children up to age 2, plan to pick them up or strap them in. Baby backpacks, baby carriers, strollers, bike trailers, and more all provide baby and parent with ample opportunity to get on the trail. Paved trails and well-maintained gravel trails all provide access to the younger set.

Children between the ages of 2 and 4 can usually hike up to 2 miles. Be sure to plan plenty of extra time and know that you may end up carrying them. Children between the ages of 5 and 7 can hike 3 to 4 miles over easy terrain. Resting, stopping, and plenty of wandering should be allowed for these age groups. Above age 8, children can easily hike a full day at a slow pace. A full day may include covering 6 miles over variable terrain. Set your entire group or family hiking goals based on the youngest child's ability. Preteens and teenagers may begin to hike more difficult trails if they have had hiking experience.

Children should be taught from the get-go that they must stay within eyesight of an adult. They are never to run off. Not only can they get lost or injured, but they also can cause damage to the trail or the ecosystem. Teach your kids to treat the outdoors kindly, and the outdoors will repay the favor.

Also teach your children to stay where they are if they do end up getting lost. Many children relate to the instruction to hug a tree when lost—tell them to find one, hold on to it, and blow their whistle. Three whistle blows is the standard distress signal, which indicates, "I am lost" or "I need help." Likewise, never let kids go close to steep cliffs and other drop-off areas. Rules about going near rivers and other water sources and climbing on accessible rocks must be addressed as well. (My rule with my kids is simply, "No!")

Always teach trail etiquette: Leave no trace, pick up after others who do not, the uphill hiker has the right of way, and don't pick or pull anything. And of course, a cautionary rhyme about poison ivy: leaves of three, let them be.

Before you leave home, have the children help make a special kid-friendly map of the area that they can keep in their bag, including a legend that has items such as waterfalls, trails, trees, or tents. Making maps helps teach direction and creativity. Draw the route and have the child mark interesting waypoints while they are hiking.

Toy stores are home to many kids' camping and hiking supplies, such as magnifying glasses, which can be used to identify plants, insects, minerals in rocks, and flowers.

Make homemade scavenger-hunt cards to use on any hike away from the campground (or in the area around the campground). Use a stack of index cards, and have your child cut hiking-related images from used magazines and paste them on each card. Or your child can draw the items. Write the name under the item and bring as many cards on your hike as you want. Some families might even want to laminate the cards. When you see one of the items on your hike, simply mark a tiny X on the back of the card instead of drawing an X across the image—that way, you'll be able to use the cards again. It's fun to have a trump card that could be tucked away for special sightings: bull snake, lost watch, or an abandoned sock. Don't forget to bring a permanent marker.

Games like "I Spy" can keep kids occupied in the outdoors, and you also can introduce them to bird-watching, look for animal tracks, or simply count rocks as you hike. The key is to play games that encourage children to observe their surroundings.

Assign one child to be the hiking leader (or mountain leader, as we call it), and have him or her guide the hike. Plan on taking a lot of breaks, and, if you're traveling with more than one child, at each break designate a new hiking leader.

Have your child invite a friend, which helps your child see the world from another youngster's perspective.

If the hike is going well, be sure to head home a little early, especially if you have to turn around and trace your steps. It is always better to end early on a positive note than to end with sore feet, a lot of whining, and discouraged hikers.

Packing

Packing for the kids is much like packing for the parents. Be sure each camper-hiker has the U.S. Forest Service's "ten essentials": compass, first-aid kit, flashlight, high-energy food, knife, map, suitable extra clothing (such as rain gear), sun protection, water, and waterproof matches, plus a mirror and a whistle. Mom and Dad may want to carry the bulk of the weight, as well as potentially dangerous items such as the knife and matches. But keep in mind that many kids enjoy the responsibility that comes with carrying part of the load, and that way parents don't have to schlep everything around.

When hiking with a stroller or other apparatus, it's easy to stash extra essentials such as diapers and baby wipes. Some other items to consider if you have extra room: your child's favorite wholesome snack, juice, sunglasses, sunscreen, baby wipes, kid's trail map, kid's magnifying glass, scavenger-hunt cards, lunch, and permanent markers.

Be sure everyone is dressed for the weather. For hot or cold days, the rule is to dress in layers. Start out with more in the winter and less in the summer. All children need to have one proper pair of socks and one proper pair of shoes. Be sure there is no cotton in the socks, since cotton retains moisture and helps create blisters. Instead, buy child-size wool socks and nylon liners. Good tennis shoes are great, and children's hiking boots are even better.

For overnight hikes, each child needs a sleeping bag that will fit his or her body type and provide warmth. Do your research on sizes and temperature ratings. (Don't cave in and get the Barbie sleeping bag little Susie really wants. Save that for slumber parties indoors.)

ROCKY MOUNTAIN NATIONAL PARK'S COMMITMENT TO KIDS

Rocky Mountain National Park offers fabulous ranger-led programs all year, geared toward kids ages 6 to 12. There are free Junior Ranger activity booklets available at the park's visitor centers. A successfully completed book earns a badge.

General Safety

- **DO NOT EVER RELY ON CELL PHONES IN THE ROCKIES.** Signals and access are very inconsistent. Check with your cellular-service provider before leaving home. Many outdoor enthusiasts still rely on GPS and other forms of communication in the backcountry.

- **ALWAYS CARRY FOOD AND WATER** whether you are planning to go overnight or not. Food will give you energy, help keep you warm, and sustain you in an emergency situation until help arrives. You never know if you will have a stream nearby when you become thirsty. Bring potable water or treat water before drinking it from a stream. Boil or filter all found water before drinking it.

- **STAY ON DESIGNATED TRAILS.** Most hikers get lost when they leave the path. Even on the most clearly marked trails, there is usually a point where you have to stop and consider which direction to head. If you become disoriented, don't panic. As soon as you think you may be off track, stop, assess your current direction, and then retrace your steps back to the point where you went awry.

Using a map, compass, this book, and keeping in mind what you have passed thus far, reorient yourself, and trust your judgment on which way to continue. If you become absolutely unsure of how to continue, return to your vehicle the way you came in. Should you become completely lost and have no idea of how to return to the trailhead, remaining in place along the trail and waiting for help is most often the best option for adults and always the best option for children.

- **BE ESPECIALLY CAREFUL WHEN YOU'RE CROSSING STREAMS.** Whether you are fording the stream or crossing on a log, make every step count. If you have any doubt about maintaining your balance on a foot log, go ahead and ford the stream instead. When fording a stream, use a trekking pole or stout stick for balance, and face upstream as you cross. If a stream seems too deep to ford, turn back. Whatever is on the other side is not worth risking your life.

- **BE CAREFUL AT OVERLOOKS.** While these areas may provide spectacular views, they are potentially hazardous. Stay back from the edge of outcrops and be absolutely sure of your footing; a misstep can mean a nasty and possibly fatal fall.

- **STANDING DEAD TREES AND STORM-DAMAGED LIVING TREES** pose a real hazard to hikers and tent campers. These trees may have loose or broken limbs that could fall at any time. When choosing a spot to rest or a backcountry campsite, look up.

- **TAKE TIME TO THINK.** A cool, calculating mind is the single most important piece of equipment you'll ever need on the trail. Think before you act. Watch your step. Plan ahead. Avoiding accidents before they happen is the best recipe for a rewarding and relaxing hike.

- **ASK QUESTIONS.** Rocky Mountain National Park employees are there to help. It's a lot easier to get advice before you start your trek than it is while you're out there.

Animal and Plant Hazards

ROCKY MOUNTAIN NATIONAL PARK has all sorts of wildlife: mule deer, bighorn sheep, coyote, elk, pika, moose, marmots, and more. Here's a quick primer on how best to enjoy watching wildlife:

- Never, ever feed wildlife.
- Watch from a distance.
- Obey all closure signs.
- Wildlife calls and spotlights are illegal in Rocky Mountain National Park.
- Drive cautiously and do not block traffic to look at wildlife.

Black Bears

There are no definite rules about what to do if you meet a bear. In most cases the bear will detect you first and leave. If you do encounter a bear, here are some suggestions from the National Park Service:

- Stay calm.
- Move away, talking loudly to alert the bear of your presence.
- Back away while facing the bear.
- Avoid eye contact.
- Give the bear plenty of room to escape; bears will rarely attack unless they are threatened or provoked.
- Don't run or make sudden movements; running will provoke the bear, and you cannot outrun it.
- Do not attempt to climb trees to escape bears, especially black bears. The animal will pull you down by the foot.
- Fight back if attacked. Black bears have been driven away when people have fought back with rocks, sticks, binoculars, and even their bare hands.
- Be grateful that it's not a grizzly bear. There are none in Rocky Mountain National Park.

Mountain Lions

Lion attacks on people are rare, with fewer than 12 fatalities in 100 years. Based on observations by people who have come in contact with mountain lions, some patterns are beginning to emerge. Below are more suggestions from the National Park Service:

- Stay calm.
- Talk firmly to the lion.
- Move slowly.
- Back up or stop; never run because lions will chase and attack.
- Raise your arms. If you are wearing a sweater or coat, open it and hold it wide.
- Pick up children to make them appear larger.
- If the lion becomes aggressive, throw rocks and large objects at it. (Never crouch down or turn your back to retrieve said objects.) This is the time to convince the lion that you are not prey and that you are a danger to it.
- Fight back and try to remain standing if you are attacked.

Ticks

Ticks like to hang out in the brush that grows along trails. They seem to be abundant in hot summer months, but you should be cautious year-round. Ticks, which are arthropods and not insects, need a host to feast on in order to reproduce. The ticks that latch onto you while hiking will be very small, sometimes so tiny that you won't be able to spot them. Primarily of two varieties, deer ticks and dog ticks, they need a few hours of attachment before they can potentially transmit any disease. Ticks may settle in shoes, socks, and hats, and may take several hours to actually latch on. The best strategy is to visually check every half-hour or so while hiking, do a thorough check before you get in the car, and then, when you take a post-hike shower, do an even more thorough check of your entire body. Ticks that haven't attached are easily removed but not easily killed. If you pick off a tick in the woods, just toss it aside. If you find one on your body at home, remove it and then send it down the toilet. For ticks that have embedded, removal with tweezers is best.

PHOTO: Jane Huber

Snakes

Rocky Mountain National Park is proud to claim that there is only one reptile species inside the park: the harmless garter snake. In any case, I like to include information on the venomous snake that is found in areas that border the park region. Rattler sightings are very common in some of those areas, so why wouldn't one be able to sneak into the park? A good rule of thumb is to give rattlers a wide berth and leave them alone. In the chance that you are bitten by a rattlesnake, stay calm and get help immediately.

Poison Ivy

Recognizing poison ivy and avoiding contact with it is the most effective way to prevent the painful, itchy rashes associated with this plant. Urushiol, the oil in the sap of poison ivy, is responsible for the rash. Usually within 12 to 14 hours of exposure (but sometimes much later), raised lines and/or blisters will appear, accompanied by a terrible itch. Refrain from scratching because bacteria under fingernails can cause infection, and you will spread the rash to other parts of your body. Wash and dry the rash thoroughly, applying calamine lotion or another product to help dry the rash. If itching or blistering is severe, seek medical attention. Remember that oil-contaminated clothes, pets, or hiking gear can easily cause an irritating rash on you or someone else, so wash not only any exposed parts of your body but also clothes, gear, and pets.

Mosquitoes

Although it's not common, individuals can become infected with the West Nile virus by being bitten by an infected mosquito. Culex mosquitoes, the primary variety that can transmit the virus to humans, thrive in urban rather than natural areas. They lay their eggs in stagnant water and can breed in any standing water that remains for more than five days. Most people infected with the West Nile virus have no symptoms of illness, although some may become ill, usually 3 to 15 days after being bitten.

In the park area, late spring and summer are when you're at the highest risk for mosquito bites and the possibility of the West Nile virus. At this time of year—and any time you expect mosquitoes to be buzzing around—you may want to wear protective clothing, such as long sleeves, long pants, and socks. Loose clothing in light colors is best. Spray clothes with insect repellent. Remember to follow the instructions on the repellent and to take extra care with children.

Pine Beetle Epidemic

Bark beetles are insects that have shaped forests for thousands of years. The effects of bark beetles are especially evident in recent years on the western side of Rocky Mountain National Park, especially in Grand County, where large areas of brown, dead trees are common. Hazard-tree mitigation is centered primarily near park facilities. Be very cautious in areas where trees that have died from the beetles are still standing.

Tips for Enjoying
Rocky Mountain National Park

- Before you go, visit the Rocky Mountain National Park website at nps.gov/romo, or call the park for an information kit at 970-586-1206. Both resources will help you get oriented with Rocky Mountain National Park.

- Most visitors arrive during the summer months. Expect a lot of company on the roads, on some of the trails, and in the parking areas, especially between Memorial Day and Labor Day.

- Elevation is an integral part of the park experience. Don't push your physical limits in this region located above 8,000 feet. Symptoms of altitude sickness include shortness of breath, fatigue, dizziness, nausea, rapid heartbeat, and insomnia.

- Upon arrival, stop by a park visitor center for current information on everything from road and weather conditions to ranger-led programs.

- There is no lodging available inside the park, but hundreds of accommodations are nearby in and around Estes Park and Grand Lake.

- Pets are not permitted on any hiking trails.
- Bikes are not permitted on any hiking trails.
- A valid Colorado fishing license is required for fishing in the park. Annual, five-day, and one-day resident and non-resident licenses are available. Licenses are sold at most sporting-goods stores.
- The park is always open, 24 hours daily all year.
- **Entrance fees:**
  - Rocky Mountain National Park Annual Pass: **$50**
  - Rocky Mountain National Park and Arapaho National Recreation Area Annual Pass: **$60**
  - One-day automobile pass for individuals and families: **$20**
  - Seven-day automobile pass for individuals and families: **$30**
  - America the Beautiful Lifetime Senior Pass: **$10** *(US citizens or permanent residents age 62 and older)*
  - America the Beautiful Lifetime Access Pass: **free** *(US residents or permanent residents with permanent disabilities)*
  - America the Beautiful Military Pass: **free** *(active duty US military personnel and dependents)*
- Trail Ridge Road usually opens for the season on Friday of Memorial Day weekend. Heavy snows typically close the road for the winter in mid- to late October.
- Old Fall River Road is usually open from early July to late September. Old Fall River Road was heavily damaged in the 2013 flood and was not open at press time.
- Bear Lake Road is open all year, but the park urges visitors to take advantage of the Bear Lake corridor shuttle bus available May 1 to October 10.

Tips for a Happy Camping Trip

THERE'S NOTHING WORSE than a bad camping trip, especially since it's so easy to have a great time. To assist with making your outing a happy one, here are some pointers.

Always strive to practice low-impact camping. Adhere to the adages, "Pack it in, pack it out," and "Take only pictures, leave only footprints." Practice "Leave No Trace" camping ethics while in the backcountry.

- **RESERVE YOUR SITE AHEAD OF TIME.** Permits are required for camping in the park's 269 designated backcountry campsites. See the extensive backcountry regulations in Appendix B: Rocky Mountain National Park Backcountry Camping Guide, on pages 188–189. There are also five large campground neighborhoods found in the park: Aspenglen, Glacier Basin, Longs Peak, Moraine Park, and Timber Creek. For more information, visit the park's website: **nps.gov/romo.**

- **PICK YOUR CAMPING BUDDIES WISELY.** A family trip is pretty straightforward, but you may want to consider excluding any grumpy relatives who don't like bugs, sunshine, or marshmallows. Make sure that everyone joining you on the trip is on the same page regarding expectations of difficulty, sleeping arrangements, and food requirements.

- **DON'T DUPLICATE EQUIPMENT** such as cooking pots and lanterns among campers in your party. Carry what you need to have a good time, but coordinate with each other so you know what each person is bringing.

- **DRESS APPROPRIATELY FOR THE SEASON.** Educate yourself on the average temperatures of the specific area you plan to visit. It may be warm at night during summer in your backyard, but up in the mountains it could be quite chilly.

- **PITCH YOUR TENT ON A LEVEL SURFACE,** preferably one that is covered with leaves, pine straw, or grass. Pitch your tent on a tarp or specially designed footprint to thwart ground moisture and to protect the tent floor. Do a little site maintenance such as picking up small rocks and sticks that can damage your tent floor and make sleep uncomfortable. If you have a separate tent rainfly but don't need it, keep it rolled up at the base of the tent in case it starts raining at midnight.

- **TAKE A SLEEPING PAD WITH YOU.** Use one that is full-length and thicker than you think you might need. This will not only keep your hips from aching on hard ground, but also will help keep you warm.

- **IF YOU ARE NOT HIKING INTO A PRIMITIVE CAMPSITE,** there is no real need to skimp on food due to weight. Plan tasty meals and bring everything you will need to prepare, cook, eat, and clean up the mess.

HIKE 30 *Tonahutu Creek Trail to Renegade Campsite to Flattop Mountain (see page 168). You'll find plenty of water features in Rocky Mountain National Park; this waterfall was spotted on the hike to the Renegade Campsite.*

- **IF YOU'RE PRONE TO USING THE BATHROOM MULTIPLE TIMES** at night, you should plan ahead. Make sure you know where you're heading—be it an outhouse, a fully plumbed facility, or just the woods—so you're not stumbling around in the dark. Keep a flashlight and any other accoutrements you may need by the tent door.

- **STANDING DEAD TREES AND STORM-DAMAGED LIVING TREES** can pose a real hazard to tent campers. These trees may have loose or broken limbs that could fall at any time. When choosing a spot to rest or a backcountry campsite, look up.

EAST SIDE OF ROCKY MOUNTAIN NATIONAL PARK

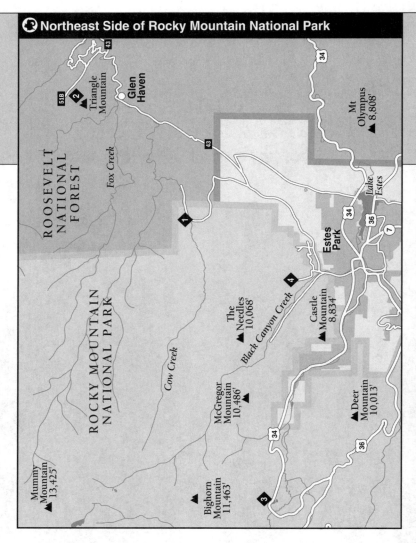

Northeast Side of Rocky Mountain National Park

51B

2

Triangle Mountain

43

Glen Haven

34

Mt Olympus 8,808'

43

Fox Creek

ROOSEVELT NATIONAL FOREST

1

Lake Estes

Estes Park

34

36

7

4

The Needles 10,068'

Castle Mountain 8,834'

Black Canyon Creek

Cow Creek

ROCKY MOUNTAIN NATIONAL PARK

McGregor Mountain 10,486'

Deer Mountain 10,013'

34

36

Mummy Mountain 13,425'

Bighorn Mountain 11,463'

3

OVERLEAF: HIKE 15 *Upper Beaver Meadows Trailhead: Ute Meadows Loop (see page 88).*

NORTHEAST SIDE OF ROCKY MOUNTAIN NATIONAL PARK
(North Fork Area and Mummy Range)

HIKE 4 *Gem Lake (see page 40). The Twin Owls are wise, old stewards of this land. A local favorite, this massive rock formation sits near Estes Park, behind the Historic Stanley Hotel.*

Cow Creek Trailhead: *Bridal Veil Falls*

SCENERY: 🌣 🌣 🌣 🌣   CHILDREN: 🌣 🌣 🌣

DIFFICULTY: 🌣 🌣 🌣   SOLITUDE: 🌣 🌣 🌣

TRAIL CONDITION: 🌣 🌣 🌣 🌣   HIKING TIME: 3½ hours

DISTANCE: 6.44 miles out-and-back

FLOOD IMPACT: 🌣 🌣 🌣 Trail conditions vary because some parts of Cow Creek were completely washed out. The trail is rugged and occasionally undefined. Expect damage on the trail. The main Bridal Veil Falls bridge was completely destroyed, but has been replaced.

OUTSTANDING FEATURES: Thundering waterfall, meadow and alpine landscape, historical ranch

A GENTLE TRAIL GIVES WAY to a strenuous push on the last portion of this uncrowded beauty. The Bridal Veil Falls crash into Cow Creek, plummeting more than 20 vertical feet from a broken rock face—the tallest falls in the park. Spring is the best time of year to visit the falls since the recent snowmelt contributes to the falls' torrent. The shoulder seasons are also nice since this is a sunny hike that can be quite warm in the summer.

From Cow Creek Trailhead at McGraw Ranch, hike west along Cow Creek Trail, which begins as a level, dirt access road. Hikers enter the ranch on foot, passing over Cow Creek, up the drive, and through the side of the ranch gate. Pass Indian Head Ranch, which is better known as Old McGraw Ranch, on the left. Pioneered and homesteaded in the 1870s, the property was later used as a cattle ranch and then as a guest ranch. The buildings, which are owned by the National Park Service, are in current use as a research and learning center accessed by universities and educational groups.

Just beyond McGraw Ranch is the junction of Cow Creek Trail with the North Boundary Trail. The rustic U.S. Forest Service–looking buildings are small in comparison to the large rock formations known as Lumpy Ridge that

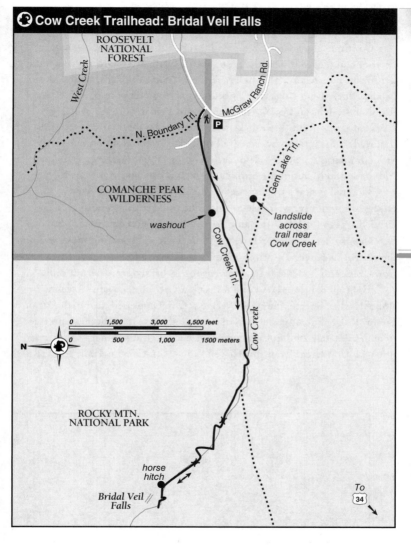

Cow Creek Trailhead: Bridal Veil Falls

West Creek

ROOSEVELT
NATIONAL
FOREST

McGraw Ranch Rd.

N. Boundary Trl.

P

COMANCHE PEAK
WILDERNESS

washout

Cow Creek Trl.

Gem Lake Trl.

landslide
across
trail near
Cow Creek

Cow Creek

0   1,500   3,000   4,500 feet
0   500   1,000   1500 meters

N

ROCKY MTN.
NATIONAL PARK

horse
hitch

Bridal Veil
Falls

To
34

dominate this area. A glasslike pond, bordered by a mountain meadow, completes the unique beginnings of this trail.

Continue along Cow Creek Trail through the open meadow, pass a restroom, and head toward the pine forest for 1.2 miles. Cross through the significant intersection of Cow Creek Trail, Bridal Veil Falls, Lawn Lake, Balance Rock, Gem Lake, and Twin Owls Parking. Take the right fork and continue straight on Cow Creek Trail toward Bridal Veil Falls, which is 2 miles from this point. Lawn Lake, another popular destination from this trailhead, is 8.1 miles away. The trail is flanked by meadows on either side, with mountains on either side of each meadow. Pine trees, spring flowers, and the sound of humming birds characterized our hike in late spring.

The trail is now a singletrack and has narrowed from the wide road. Hikers can no longer walk side by side. The trail gently ascends, and Cow Creek drops to the left. After another 0.2 mile, pass the turnoff to Rabbit Ears Campsite on the left. Above the trail, the rock formation shows you how the site got its name. The campsite is located in a secluded, shaded area near Cow Creek and is available to a small group by backcountry permit only.

The trail continues west and joins Cow Creek once again, traveling along its edge. Sheep Mountain overlooks Cow Creek and the north side of Lumpy Ridge. Sometimes technical rock climbers visit its sheer, south face. At approximately 2 miles from the trailhead, arrive at another trail intersection with Cow Creek Trail, Bridal Veil Falls, Black Canyon Trail, and Lawn

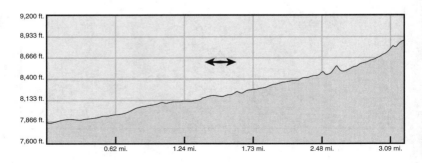

Lake Trail. Head right as the trail exits the meadow and begins a more gradual ascent into the forest.

The trail gets steeper, and for the last section, hikers cross over Cow Creek a few times via man-made bridges. The forest becomes dense and the trail becomes narrow and rocky. The next trail waypoint is a hitch rack for horses, which signifies that the last portion of the trail is inaccessible to them. Hikers will see why as they traverse over steep rock slabs and into a narrow gorge. The trail is not marked well from this point, so pay attention to your footing, the foot path, and the cairns that signify turns in the trail. The sound from the falls also will be your guide. As it gets louder and the creek becomes wilder, you will be getting closer.

After climbing a set of man-made stone steps, hikers arrive at Bridal Veil Falls, a name that suggests a vision of a bridal hairpiece that is mysterious and flowing, not unlike the falls themselves. The thundering water hitting the base of rocks and sending a spray of mist is always a crowd-pleaser—especially if the only crowd is your hiking group. Hike above the falls if you want to see the upper part of the falls and a close-up of the steep wall that forms the main section of the falls. Find a nice picnic spot, rest, and then turn around and travel back to the trailhead the way that you came.

DIRECTIONS   From Estes Park, take US 34 until it intersects Big Thompson Avenue/Elkhorn Avenue and turns into Wonderview Avenue. Pass the Stanley Historic District and take the first right onto MacGregor Avenue. Travel 3.5 miles from MacGregor Ranch Road, and then take a left at McGraw Ranch Road. Continue for 2.5 miles to the trailhead; parallel park in designated areas only.

GPS TRAILHEAD COORDINATES
N40°25.743' W105°29.998'

2 Dunraven Trailhead:
North Fork Trail to Happily Lost Campsite

SCENERY: ✿ ✿ ✿ ✿

DIFFICULTY: ✿ ✿ ✿ ✿

TRAIL CONDITION: ✿ ✿

CHILDREN: ✿

SOLITUDE: ✿ ✿ ✿ ✿ ✿

HIKING TIME: 7 hours

DISTANCE: 12.5 miles out-and-back

FLOOD IMPACT: ✿ ✿ ✿ Access to Dunraven Trailhead was closed for some time but has been reopened by the U.S. Forest Service. Driving through Dunraven is sobering and a reminder of the flood impact on Rocky Mountain National Park communities. There is still damage on the trail, but all necessary bridges have been repaired.

OUTSTANDING FEATURES: Remote, lesser used part of the park, dense forest, follows river most of the way, soft trail

THE TRAIL TO HAPPILY LOST is unique to this book. Like its namesake, the trail leaves you feeling lost in the wilderness: remoteness, variety, and density define the experience. This is a great trail for a hot summer day. The campsite is very private and very hidden. The forest is so dense here that we cannot say enough about its "Black Forest" appeal. After the first mile, you do cross through civilization at Camp Cheley, but it passes quickly.

🚶🚶 Leave the trailhead and follow the North Fork Trail as it travels up a short rise and then begins a sharp descent to the North Fork of the Big Thompson River. At the sign directing hikers toward Rocky Mountain National Park, take a right turn. Hike along the river while noting spots to stop and cool your feet on the return trip. There are a lot of pools and eddies in this first leg of the North Fork. The trail is narrow along the river.

Hike up the ravine where the trail is lush, green, and seemingly in its own world. Begin to cross a series of large wooden bridges that cross back and forth across the North Fork. Approach what might appear to be a large luxury log home, until you notice the horse corral, basketball court, and archery

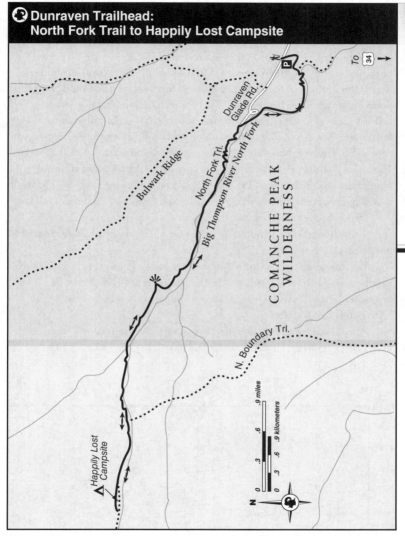

Dunraven Trailhead:
North Fork Trail to Happily Lost Campsite

To 34

P

Dunraven Glade Rd.

North Fork Trl.

Bulwark Ridge

Big Thompson River North Fork

COMANCHE PEAK WILDERNESS

N. Boundary Trl.

Happily Lost Campsite

.9 miles

.6

.9 kilometers

.3

.6

0   .3

N

range. This is a branch of the famed Cheley Camp. In my younger days, I camped at their main lodges off Marys Lake Road.

Pass the horse shed and corral, cross the bridge, and start to leave the camp behind. The trail joins with a short stretch of narrow road that's part of the camp. The trail then turns to soft, deep sand, which requires a little more effort going up, but feels nice on tired feet when you're coming back down. Time for more bridges, and then the terrain opens up a little bit as the ravine widens to a valley. There is a view now, but it is slightly obscured by the lodgepole-pine forest. Continue to another bridge; before you cross it you will spot a U.S. Forest Service campsite. Do not confuse these sites with the Rocky Mountain National Park campsites. They are totally separate and sit in the Comanche Peak Wilderness. Pass another campsite after the bridge. The trail makes an abrupt change to a narrow, hard-packed dirt path, but it doesn't last.

Cross through the meadow, lined with stately ponderosa pine trees. At this point, hikers will encounter a steeper trail. The second half of the trail has the most elevation gain.

Pass the remains of a cabin, left over from an old hunting resort, appropriately named Deserted Village. On the left are more U.S. Forest Service campsites. Cross a small stream and continue across another meadow past U.S. Forest Service campsite 9.

After traveling in a straight line for some time, the trail has an uncharacteristic switchback. Head northeast and away from the water for a change.

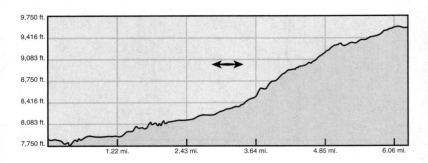

Pay attention to the trail because the path is steep and hard to follow. Stop at a nice resting spot on the rocks, complete with views.

Pass through the boundary to Rocky Mountain National Park. A higher standard of trail maintenance exists here and is evident from the start. The log stairs and erosion devices make it obvious. Rejoin the river at the small cascade on the left. Continue, passing a few campsites and the intersection with the North Boundary Trail. Enter a lichen-draped forest. Pass the Kettle Tarn Campsite and the Halfway Campsite. Halfway earned its namesake because it is located at half the elevation gain for those hiking to Lost Lake. At this point you've gained 1,400 feet from the trailhead. We continue another 0.9 mile and 200 feet of elevation to the Happily Lost Campsite. Go left into the campsite and follow the red marker signs into the dense forest. The trail winds to the right, and it is there that you spot the silver arrow that marks the designated campsite. Two small tent sites and a little fire pit are located 100 feet from the river. There are some views peeking out from the shelter of the forest. On the other side of the main trail is the privy. This campsite offers a deep-woods experience, situated in a cool, dark forest. Be sure to set up camp early and forego the scary campfire stories for the night. Have a nice rest, and in the morning, head back the way that you came.

DIRECTIONS   Take US 34 west from Loveland for 17 miles to Drake. Turn right on CR 43 and travel 6 miles to CR 518, past the Glen Haven Post Office and the sign that says FOREST ACCESS 2¼ MILES. Turn left onto the dirt road and drive 2.25 miles to the parking lot and trailhead.

GPS TRAILHEAD COORDINATES
N40°28.418' W105°27.597'

3 Lawn Lake Trailhead:
Ypsilon Trail to Upper Chipmunk Campsite

SCENERY: ☆ ☆ ☆ ☆

CHILDREN: ☆ ☆

DIFFICULTY: ☆ ☆ ☆ ☆

SOLITUDE: ☆ ☆ ☆

TRAIL CONDITION: ☆ ☆ ☆ ☆

HIKING TIME: 5 hours

DISTANCE: 8.4 miles out-and-back

FLOOD IMPACT: ☆ ☆ ☆ ☆ Lawn Lake and Ypsilon Lake Trails have significant damage, with sections of trail that are completely missing. Significant erosion of the banks of the Roaring River during the flood took out several sections of the trail. The Ypsilon Trail starts 1.4 miles up the Lawn Lake Trail. At the trail junction, the Ypsilon Lake Trail branches to the west and crosses the Roaring River. The portion of the trail and bridge that crosses the Roaring River washed out during the flood, so access is very difficult during high water. The Ypsilon Trail does not continue to follow the Roaring River at this point, and the remaining flood damage is up trail on Lawn Lake Trail and not featured in this book.

OUTSTANDING FEATURES: Horseshoe Falls, Chipmunk Lake, Ypsilon Mountain, Ypsilon Lake, forest, Roaring River

THIS HIKE IS FULL OF DRAMA: the Y-shaped, snow-filled scar on Ypsilon Mountain; Horseshoe Falls and the canyon gorged by the escaped dam waters of Lawn Lake; and the lung-busting climb of the Ypsilon Trail. You'll be widely entertained—not to mention sufficiently tired—at the end of this hike to the Upper Chipmunk Campsite, which is located between Chipmunk Lake and Ypsilon Lake and provides access to both.

🚶🚶 Leave the trailhead and start on Lawn Lake Trail. Go up the man-made stairs and continue to the first major intersection of Ypsilon Lake, Lawn Lake, and Deer Mountain Trails. Turn left here. The next junction is an intersection with a horse trail; stay straight. The trail travels at a slight ascent; it's sandy and full of rocks.

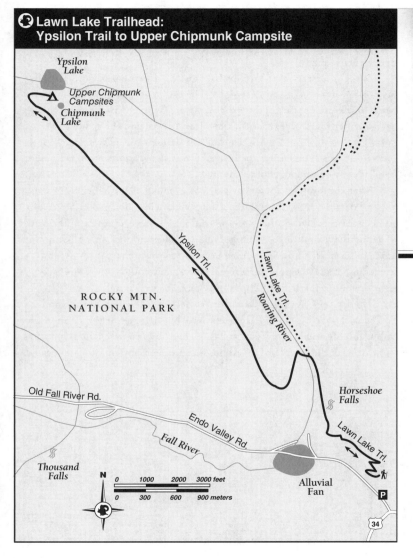

Lawn Lake Trailhead:
Ypsilon Trail to Upper Chipmunk Campsite

Ypsilon Lake

Upper Chipmunk Campsites

Chipmunk Lake

Ypsilon Trl.

ROCKY MTN.
NATIONAL PARK

Lawn Lake Trl.

Roaring River

Old Fall River Rd.

Horseshoe Falls

Lawn Lake Trl.

Endo Valley Rd.

Fall River

Thousand Falls

Alluvial Fan

N

| 0 | 1000 | 2000 | 3000 feet |
| 0 | 300 | 600 | 900 meters |

P

34

The hike continues with a series of switchbacks. After a half mile the trail passes along Horseshoe Falls and the Alluvial Fan of mud, sand, and boulders that swept down into Horseshoe Park when the 1982 Lawn Lake flood forged its destructive path.

At the intersection of Ypsilon Lake and the Lawn Lake Trail, take a left turn following the Ypsilon Lake signs. The trail is very sandy and almost beach-like as it approaches the Roaring River. Cross the river on a split-log bridge. After the bridge, cross into the forest and begin the arduous trek uphill. It's an unforgiving hill that offers only a few restful switchbacks at the very end. The steepest areas are secured by log steps, and the trail is lined on both sides by dense lodgepole-pine trees.

After climbing for the better part of 2.5 miles, the trail begins to level out and descend. Ahead are the first spectacular views of Ypsilon Mountain and her formidable, southeast facing couloir. A long 4 miles from the trailhead and the beginning of the hike, you pass the southwest side of Chipmunk Lake. It is a small alpine lake, lined by boulders and a marshy shore, and framed by large lodgepole-pine trees. Pass a giant boulder field and take a right turn onto the Upper Chipmunk Campsite access trail.

The Upper Chipmunk Campsite is another 0.2 mile into the woods. You cannot see Chipmunk Lake from here, but there are tree-obscured views of Ypsilon Mountain and Ypsilon Lake. There are two designated campsites and a privy in the middle of the woods with no shelter. The sites are located

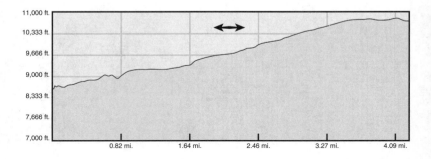

in a dense pine forest on the edge of the Ypsilon Lake drainage. This is a great place to rest for the night or to have a nice private picnic.

No trip to the Upper Chipmunk Campsite would be complete without a visit to the shore of Ypsilon Lake. Be sure to make a side trip down the trail as it descends sharply and then climbs a little, and then descends again to Ypsilon Lake. You will pass the waterfalls from neighboring lakes. The trail skirts the lake along most of its shore, except for the dramatic rise of Ypsilon Mountain on the northwest shore.

Whether camping or day hiking, trace your way back to Chipmunk Lake and then head back to the trailhead the way that you came.

DIRECTIONS From the Beaver Meadows Entrance, take US 36 west to the intersection of US 36 and US 34. Turn right onto US 34 and travel 1.8 miles to the turn for Old Fall River Road. Turn left onto Old Fall River Road, and then take a right into the Lawn Lake Trailhead parking lot.

GPS TRAILHEAD COORDINATES
N40°24.317' W105°37.525'

4 Lumpy Ridge Trailhead: *Gem Lake*

SCENERY: ✿ ✿ ✿ ✿

DIFFICULTY: ✿ ✿ ✿

TRAIL CONDITION: ✿ ✿ ✿ ✿

CHILDREN: ✿ ✿ ✿

SOLITUDE: ✿ ✿ ✿

HIKING TIME: 2½ hours

DISTANCE: 3.4 miles out-and-back

FLOOD IMPACT: ✿ Damage is primarily limited to North Gem Lake Trail and areas beyond Gem Lake.

OUTSTANDING FEATURES: Views of Estes Park, Rocky Mountain National Park, Twin Owls, alpine lake

GEM LAKE, if you'll pardon the pun, is a jewel. Located on the eastern edge of Rocky Mountain National Park, this trailhead is one of the closest to the town of Estes Park.

To begin this hike, leave your car and walk to the trailhead and signs that mark the beginning of the Gem Lake Trail. Gem Lake's lower elevation in relation to the rest of Rocky Mountain National Park, along with the hike's southern exposure, make this a great year-round hike. Estes Park is home to retirees, families, and other outdoors enthusiasts, so both the very old and very young frequent this trail.

In 2007, the Twin Owls and Gem Lake Trailheads were combined and renamed the Lumpy Ridge Trailhead. Until then, the trails split the crowds pretty evenly, so access to Gem Lake may be a little more crowded than it had been in the past. You're also hiking a trail that is 0.3 mile shorter than those I have featured in previous books.

In a few yards a steady climb begins, supplemented by short switchbacks that weave in and out of the trees and skirt around large rocks. After 0.5 mile, the Gem Lake Trail reaches a junction with the trail that leads west to the Twin Owls—massive rock formations that resemble two giant owls resting

🌀 Lumpy Ridge Trailhead: Gem Lake

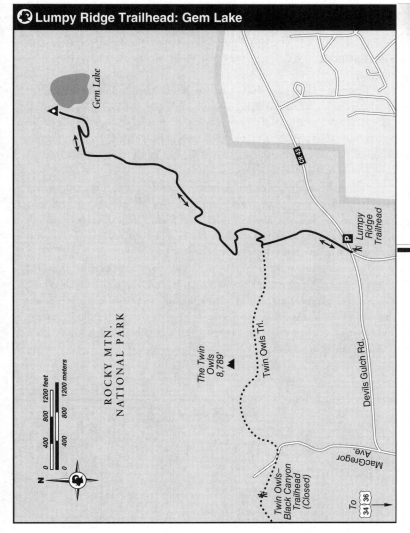

Gem Lake

CR 43

Lumpy Ridge Trailhead

P

ROCKY MTN.
NATIONAL PARK

The Twin
Owls
8,789'

Twin Owls Trl.

Devils Gulch Rd.

Twin Owls-
Black Canyon
Trailhead
(Closed)

MacGregor Ave.

To
34 36

N

0   400   800   1200 feet
0   400   800   1200 meters

on the crest of the hill. This intersection mostly marks access for rock climbers and their left turn to the owls, which you can see as you access the trailhead by car (a good point of reference is to look behind the Stanley Hotel). The climbing here is very technical, and climbers observe a strict code of conduct.

Staying on Gem Lake Trail, turn right (east) and follow the trail as it climbs moderately. To the right, catch the first views of Rocky Mountain National Park and one of its more famous mountains: Longs Peak, a popular fourteener—what a peak of 14,000 feet or higher is called. You can find the mountain by looking for the silhouette of a beaver climbing up the side of a hill. The peak is at the beaver's nose.

Follow the sandy footpath near where heavy foot traffic has cut many random paths to scenic overlooks. Continue over smooth rock outcroppings and take in the views of Lake Estes and Estes Park. The trail veers to the left and becomes even softer and sandier. On one of my hikes here, I saw a young racked buck, a rare sight this close to town.

Descend into a small, rocky canyon where you find a bench and Paul Bunyan's Boot. Another rock formation of legend, this one resembles an outsize boot propped on its heel. (Note the hole in the sole.) Continue up the many switchbacks, passing a precariously placed outhouse along the way. This portion of the trail is quite narrow and navigates through a large boulder field and granite slabs.

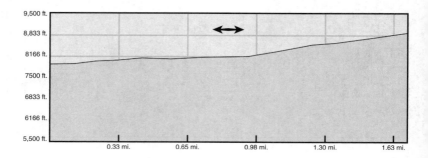

Gem Lake comes into view at the base of granite cliffs with boulders and a small beach at the water's edge. This mountain lake is a bit cold for the body, but a few minutes' respite here will cleanse the soul. When the sun hits the water, you'll see the mix of jewel tones—emerald, sapphire, ruby, and diamond—that gives the lake its name.

To return to the trailhead, head back the way you came. If you have more time, there are plenty of hikes that continue past Gem Lake and venture for hours, if not days, into Rocky Mountain National Park.

DIRECTIONS   From Estes Park, take US 34 until it intersects Big Thompson Avenue/Elkhorn Avenue and turns into Wonderview Avenue. Pass the Stanley Historic District and take the first right onto MacGregor Avenue. Follow MacGregor as it veers right and turns into Devils Gulch Road, and follow it until you reach the Lumpy Ridge Trailhead turnoff on the left.

GPS TRAILHEAD COORDINATES
N40°24.012' W105°31.397'

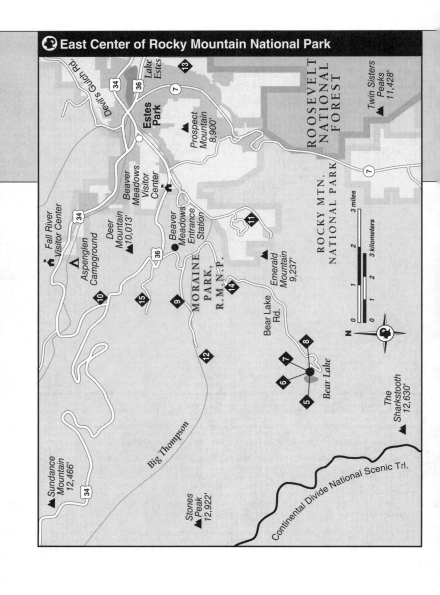

East Center of Rocky Mountain National Park

EAST CENTER
OF ROCKY MOUNTAIN
NATIONAL PARK
(Gorge Lakes Area and Bear Lake Area)

HIKE 15 *Ute Meadows Loop (see page 88); Upper Beaver Meadows*

5 Bear Lake Trailhead: *Bierstadt Lake*

SCENERY: ✪ ✪ ✪

DIFFICULTY: ✪ ✪

TRAIL CONDITION: ✪ ✪ ✪ ✪

DISTANCE: 5 miles out-and-back

FLOOD IMPACT: **0**

OUTSTANDING FEATURES: Aspen trees, mountain lake

CHILDREN: ✪ ✪ ✪

SOLITUDE: ✪ ✪

HIKING TIME: 2½ hours

FOUR MAIN TRAILS SERVICE Bierstadt Lake. Bear Lake Trailhead is an easier, longer option because the trailhead is slightly higher than the subalpine lake destination. So instead of heading up and away, you can treat yourself to a gradual descent with a worthy reward. The up part can come at the end this time.

From the Bear Lake Trailhead, follow the masses past the entrance to the Bear Lake hikes. Of all the paths at this trailhead, this one is the easiest to find—being a popular winter cross-country skiing trail, it's marked with orange fluorescent squares.

From here, follow the Flattop Mountain Trail, which heads to Odessa Lake, for approximately 0.4 mile to the intersection of Bierstadt Lake Trail.

Bierstadt Lake was named after Albert Bierstadt, a famous 19th-century painter. He's most renowned for the large canvases that he sold to royalty, paintings portraying the West and the landscapes of the Rockies. One such depiction of Estes Park and Longs Peak was commissioned by the Earl of Dunraven, who took it to Europe to hang in the Dunraven Castle.

Continue straight toward Bierstadt Lake. The trail up to this point is characterized by a small climb through the trees, both aspen and pine. As promised, the trail now descends along an easy, wooded path for 0.75 mile

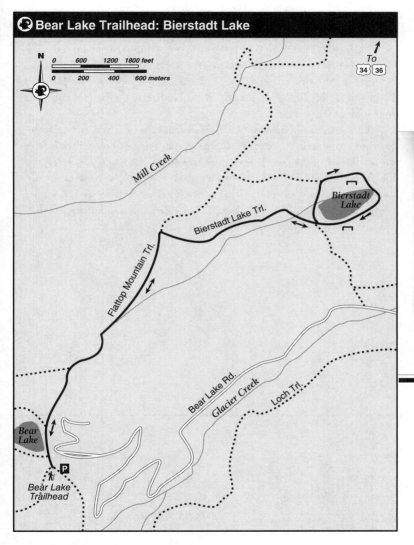

N

0   600   1200   1800 feet

0   200   400   600 meters

Mill Creek

Bierstadt Lake Trl.

Flattop Mountain Trl.

Bierstadt Lake

GORGE LAKES AREA
AND BEAR LAKE AREA

To
34 36

Bear Lake Rd.

Glacier Creek

Loch Trl.

Bear Lake

P

Bear Lake Trailhead

to the intersection of Bierstadt Lake Trial, Mill Creek Basin, and Hollowell Park. Continue straight.

The next intersection is with the loop trail around Bierstadt Lake where hikers continue straight and begin a clockwise circle around the lake. Another intersection passes quickly and it is another meeting with Mill Creek Basin and Hollowell Park to the left. Keep heading to the right to complete your loop of the lake.

The picturesque Bierstadt Lake offers fabulous views that stretch from Notchtop Mountain to Longs Peak. The optimal view of Longs Peak is from the north side of the lake. Due to thick tree cover, the lake is very rarely visible from the trail around it. Hikers must take various spur trails or social trails to get to the lake's shore. There are a few small beaches perfect for a picnic or rest. The shallowest edges of the lake are filled with plant life that grows in and out of the water.

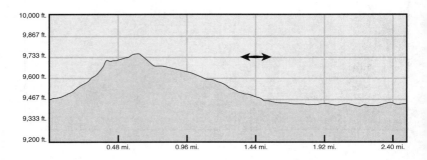

Continue heading right at the intersection with the Bierstadt Lake Trailhead trail. This trail is a shorter, more difficult hike that zigzags 1.4 miles up the south side of Bierstadt Moraine from the Bierstadt Lake Trailhead. One option, during the shuttle bus season, is to take the Bierstadt Lake Trail down to the Bierstadt Lake Trailhead on Bear Lake Road and take the shuttle bus back to your car at the Bear Lake Trailhead.

If you are going to stick to the original plan, when you get back to the beginning of the loop, turn left and head back the way you came to the Bear Lake Trailhead.

DIRECTIONS   From Estes Park go to Rocky Mountain National Park's Beaver Meadows Entrance Station via US 36. After entering the park, go 0.2 mile, take a left at Bear Lake Road, and travel 9.3 miles to the Bear Lake Trailhead parking lot.

GPS TRAILHEAD COORDINATES
N40°18.614' W105°38.724'

6 Bear Lake Trailhead: *Emerald Lake*

SCENERY: ✿ ✿ ✿ ✿	CHILDREN: ✿ ✿ ✿
DIFFICULTY: ✿ ✿ ✿	SOLITUDE: ✿
TRAIL CONDITION: ✿ ✿ ✿	HIKING TIME: 2 hours

DISTANCE: 3.6 miles out-and-back

FLOOD IMPACT: 0

OUTSTANDING FEATURES: Three mountain lakes, alpine forest, variety of streams

HERE YOU GET THREE LAKES for the price of one. Add in Bear Lake, and that's four lakes for the price of one. The lakes are all unique and spaced apart nicely to keep hikers interested. Because of the obvious value of this hike, it can be very crowded. Even in late spring, you'll traverse snow.

🚶‍♂️ Leave Bear Lake Trailhead. At the trail mileage sign for Emerald Lake 1.8 miles, take a left turn. When we hiked in spring, the wide beginnings of this trail were packed with people. At the next fork, take a right turn, heading up the hill.

The trail is composed of rough asphalt. Continue to travel at a slight ascent. The trail is framed by pine and aspen trees. Views of the mountain ranges are to your left, and a hillside is immediately to the right.

Your first destination, Nymph Lake, comes up quickly after 0.5 mile. In early June, snow still flanks its edges. The lake is deep, dark blue, and calm, with only the pine forest reflected in its mirror. Lily pads float on its surface in the summer. The trail continues to head up and around the back of Nymph Lake. Cross through a boulder field, descend for a short time, and then continue. The path is no longer asphalt and is instead a soft, dirt-packed singletrack. In the summer, expect to cross through small streams and marshy spots full of mountain wildflowers. Flattop Mountain, Hallett

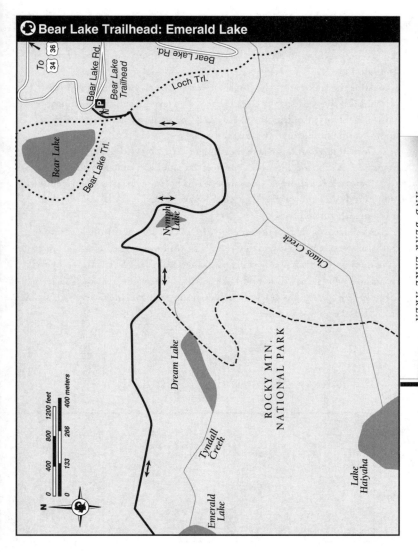

GORGE LAKES AREA
AND BEAR LAKE AREA

To 34 36

Bear Lake Rd.

Bear Lake Rd.

Loch Trl.

Bear Lake Trailhead

Bear Lake

Bear Lake Trl.

Nymph Lake

Chaos Creek

Dream Lake

ROCKY MTN.
NATIONAL PARK

Tyndall Creek

Emerald Lake

Lake Haiyaha

0   400   800   1200 feet

0   133   266   400 meters

N

Peak, and Longs Peak are all in view from the trail at one point or another. While the lakes share similar backdrops, they are all unique and range from the lushness of Nymph Lake to the serenity of Dream Lake to the drama of Emerald Lake.

After the trail enters the forest and takes hikers through a few steep switchbacks, the next stop is Dream Lake. The lake's open shores appear to consume the surrounding forest and rock formations, giving it an almost surreal or dreamlike quality—thus the name.

Continue around the lake, heading toward Emerald Lake. The trail to Emerald Lake follows the north shore of Dream Lake and then climbs over rocks before it levels out. Conditions at this point, especially when we hiked, were muddy and snowpacked, which discouraged many of the crowds that subsequently turned back.

After passing the northwest edge of Dream Lake, continue to climb the trail along the banks of Tyndall Creek. The trail passes through the forest and continues up the man-made staircase along a waterfall. Surrounded by rock spires and talus slopes, Emerald Lake is truly a scenic destination. When we hiked in late spring, the tracks from backcountry snow riders were still visible from the lake's sloped shores.

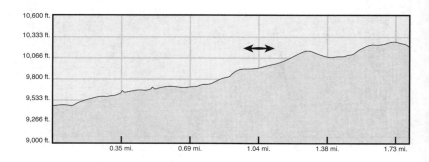

Tyndall Gorge rises to the west and into the Continental Divide. From here you also can see the north face of Hallett Peak and the south side of Flattop Mountain. Steep rock walls on all sides, except for the side that hosts the trail, offer no escape—not that you need one! (However, there was a moment during my hike when I thought we might need a quick escape: A chipmunk climbed up the back of my husband, Bruce, and he gave me quite a scare when he screamed for his life!)

After a quick respite on one of the sunbaked boulders at the end of the trail, turn around and go back to the trailhead the same way you came.

DIRECTIONS   From Estes Park go to Rocky Mountain National Park's Beaver Meadows Entrance Station via US 36. After entering the park, go 0.2 mile, take a left at Bear Lake Road, and travel 9.3 miles to the Bear Lake Trailhead parking lot.

GPS TRAILHEAD COORDINATES
N40°18.614' W105°38.724'

7 Bear Lake Trailhead: *Flattop Mountain*

SCENERY: ✿ ✿ ✿ ✿ ✿   CHILDREN: ✿

DIFFICULTY: ✿ ✿ ✿ ✿ ✿   SOLITUDE: ✿ ✿ ✿

TRAIL CONDITION: ✿ ✿ ✿ ✿   HIKING TIME: 6 hours

DISTANCE: 8.8 miles out-and-back   (going approximately 1½ mph)

FLOOD IMPACT: **0**

OUTSTANDING FEATURES: Timberline, views of alpine lakes, tundra, summit hike

---

FLATTOP MOUNTAIN IS A LARGE, flat summit space that offers access to the Continental Divide and the trails that crisscross from Estes Park to Grand Lake. It is a well-known hike and a strenuous one—ask any locals about their last time at Flattop and they'll probably groan and talk about how sore their legs were after the trek. The trail is well maintained even though it travels through timberline and alpine tundra. The crowds of Bear Lake disappear quickly as the long alpine climb (almost 3,000 feet elevation gain!) takes shape.

🥾 From the Bear Lake parking lot, follow the sign pointing hikers to Bear Lake along a nicely appointed trail, complete with railings lining the side. At the sign for Flattop Mountain, take a right turn and begin to head uphill. The trail is now unpaved and travels through a dense aspen grove above Bear Lake. This smooth, hard-packed dirt path is wide and very well maintained, and it starts a slight grade that will be commonplace, if not steeper, for the next 4 miles. Continue to follow the signs to Flattop Mountain. A fork in the trail appears right away; the right turn goes to Bierstadt Lake, but go left to continue on the trail, still climbing.

A little less than a mile from Bear Lake is another major trail intersection. Take a hard left onto a steep switchback. The trail to the right goes to Odessa Lake and Fern Lake. The trail to Flattop Mountain continues to switchback in a zigzag pattern, traveling uphill in a very rocky, hard-packed

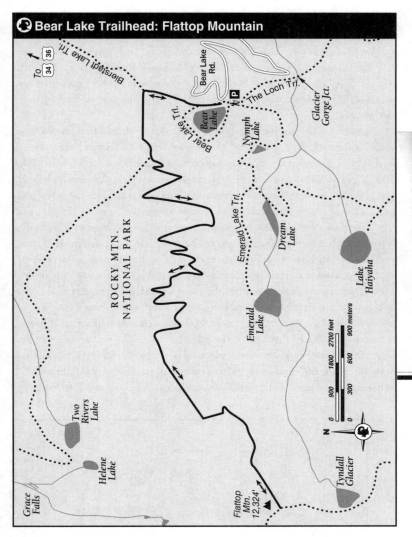

Bear Lake Trailhead: Flattop Mountain

To 34 36

Bierstadt Lake Trl.

Bear Lake Rd.

Bear Lake Trl.

Bear Lake

P

Nymph Lake

The Loch Trl.

Glacier Gorge Jct.

ROCKY MTN. NATIONAL PARK

Emerald Lake Trl.

Dream Lake

Lake Haiyaha

Emerald Lake

Two Rivers Lake

Helene Lake

Grace Falls

Flattop Mtn. 12,324'

Tyndall Glacier

0 900 1800 2700 feet
0 300 600 900 meters

N

GORGE LAKES AREA AND BEAR LAKE AREA

part of the trail. The rockiness is typical of the remainder of the trail, and many hikers at this point realize that they need to reevaluate the hike, find that they are not up to the elevation gain and grade, and turn around.

For the next 1.5 miles, several long switchbacks usher hikers up the steep terrain. They are so long that it's difficult to recognize the true nature of the switchback. They are not your customary swing-and-loop, back-and-forth switchbacks.

The trail takes you southwest, back northwest, and then back southwest again, and eventually hikers arrive at a very well-marked Dream Lake overlook. Up to this point, Longs Peak has been prominent on the left side of the hike. Views of Mills Lake and the area across Glacier Gorge, the valley below Longs Peak, are prominent. The mountain that seems to come into view every now and then is also very visible here. It is the dramatic, angular Hallett Peak.

This completes the first half of the hike. It's characterized by a grade that is consistently unrelenting and uphill. The trail travels through pine, spruce, and fir trees, with views here and there on the switchbacks and in the trees.

Some hikes exit treeline abruptly; this one takes its time, with the trees slowly getting shorter and stunted—the twisted growth, also known as krummholz, will be visible along the trail for a while. After a mile, you'll finally pass treeline and enter the tundra. The miscellaneous switchbacks that have been crisscrossing all throughout the hike continue. The rocky terrain gets a little more challenging, and eventually hikers will come to a series of switchbacks where the last turn in the series rewards hikers with a tremendous and well-marked overlook of Emerald Lake far below. The sign says DO NOT

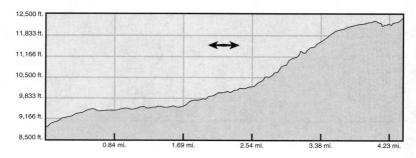

DESCEND, an obvious warning since the lake is looming 1,300 feet below, and one you should take seriously, since fatal accidents are possible, especially during snowstorms. The area in view is also known as Tyndall Gorge. Longs Peak is prominent to your left, as well as during most of the time spent above treeline. You cannot see the Flattop Mountain summit—not yet.

Looking behind, you can see Sprague Lake, the road up toward Bear Lake, and Bierstadt Lake sitting in a slight depression on top of a mountain a little closer. Scamper over rock piles arranged in various jumbles—hopping around much like the mountain pikas you're likely to see in this area. These active mammals have round ears and are about the size of rabbits. Even if you don't see them, you will most likely hear their little peeps and squeaks.

Big Valley is to the right, ending in giant granite cliffs. You will hit a long traverse heading west and up to Flattop Mountain. Eventually the trail goes over a ridge, and you can finally see part of Flattop Mountain—not a distinct peak, but instead the flat top that stretches out in front of you. The hike steepens for the last mile, crossing a rock field up near the top, and then the long plateau of Flattop Mountain is obvious.

Those wanting to continue can go up another 0.6 mile to the summit of the distinct peak to the left: Hallett Peak. For information on where this trail connects and how to get all the way to the Grand Lake side, refer to my write-up on the overnight hike, Green Mountain Trailhead: Tonahutu Creek Trail to Renegade Campsite to Flattop Mountain (page 168). Otherwise, take a quick rest, turn around (to avoid any dangers above treeline: lightning, poor visibility, and more), and go back down to Bear Lake the way that you came.

DIRECTIONS From Estes Park go to Rocky Mountain National Park's Beaver Meadows Entrance Station via US 36. After entering the park, go 0.2 mile, take a left at Bear Lake Road, and travel 9.3 miles to the Bear Lake Trailhead parking lot.

GPS TRAILHEAD COORDINATES
N40°18.614' W105°38.724'

8 Bear Lake Trailhead: *The Loch*

SCENERY: ✪ ✪ ✪ ✪ ✪   CHILDREN: ✪ ✪ ✪

DIFFICULTY: ✪ ✪ ✪   SOLITUDE: ✪ ✪ ✪

TRAIL CONDITION: ✪ ✪ ✪ ✪   HIKING TIME: 3 hours

DISTANCE: 5.4 miles out-and-back

FLOOD IMPACT: 0

OUTSTANDING FEATURES: Waterfalls, alpine lake, views

THE LOCH IS A BEAUTIFUL mountain lake that's easy to access and popular to photograph. The scenic trail takes hikers past Alberta Falls and away from the Bear Lake and Glacier Gorge Trailhead crowds. The trail can get very warm, so this is a good hike to do when it is overcast or a little bit cool.

🚶🚶   From the Bear Lake Trailhead, cross the wooden bridge and take a left turn. The trail is paved and heads downhill. After about 100 yards, take another left and the trail gradually turns to dirt, but it is so well maintained that you never really notice the difference. After a while, Bear Lake Road is visible on the left, across the river.

Bear right uphill as the trails intersect, and follow the signs to Alberta Falls. Stop at the overlook of Alberta Falls, or continue to follow the trail uphill to get better views. Social paths lead down to the left to views of various cascades as the trail follows the creek. Stay on the main trail, traveling uphill, and then stand above the falls. Hikers are treated to more cascades tumbling down to the left. Alberta Falls are gorgeous and some of the most accessible in Rocky Mountain National Park. Jeweled waters and a narrow gorge make Alberta Falls a beautiful place to visit. Eventually the trail moves away from Glacier Creek, and the views open up to the Mummy Range.

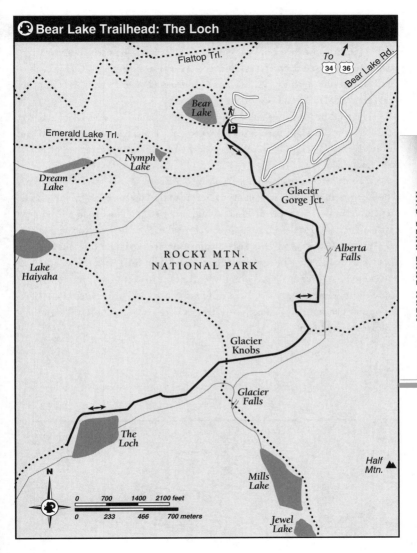

Bear Lake Trailhead: The Loch

Flattop Trl.

To
34 36

Bear Lake Rd.

Bear
Lake

P

Emerald Lake Trl.

Nymph
Lake

Dream
Lake

Glacier
Gorge Jct.

Alberta
Falls

ROCKY MTN.
NATIONAL PARK

Lake
Haiyaha

Glacier
Knobs

Glacier
Falls

The
Loch

N

Mills
Lake

Half
Mtn.

| 0 | 700 | 1400 | 2100 feet |
| 0 | 233 | 466 | 700 meters |

Jewel
Lake

At the next trail junction, bear right and go uphill, following the signs to Mill's Lake and Loch Vale. The cliffs of Glacier Knob are to the right. The trail begins to traverse an old rockslide, which is fairly exposed, but travels back into the shade of the trees. At the intersection with North Longs Peak Trail, follow the signs to The Loch and Andrews Glacier. The trail is smooth and level, passing in and out of the pine forest.

The trail drops into a subalpine bowl; here Loch Vale and Glacier Gorge come together. A right turn takes hikers to Lake Haiyaha, and the trail to the left leads into Glacier Gorge. We stay on the middle trail that leads uphill into Loch Vale.

Take the ascending switchbacks above Icy Brook and arrive at The Loch. The Loch is an alpine lake with crystal-clear water, surrounded by snow and views on all sides, with Taylor Peak taking center stage. The broad cliff at The Loch is Cathedral Wall, a favorite for technical rock climbers. To the right are Andrews Glacier and Otis Peak. Stop at the piece of land that juts out from The Loch's edge to rest, have lunch, and then turn back the way that you came. This area is a good jumping-off point for those wanting to continue on to Timberline Falls, Lake of Glass, Sky Pond, and Andrews Glacier. A popular backcountry campsite, Andrews Creek, is 0.6 mile farther up the trail from The Loch.

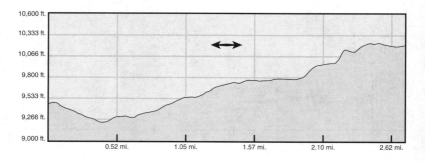

The Loch is just one of the many rewards on this spectacular trail, and it's a great place to stop for lunch before the hike back. Pictured here are the Loch and Cathedral Wall.

DIRECTIONS From Estes Park go to Rocky Mountain National Park's Beaver Meadows Entrance Station via US 36. After entering the park, go 0.2 mile, take a left at Bear Lake Road, and travel 9.3 miles to the Bear Lake Trailhead parking lot.

GPS TRAILHEAD COORDINATES
N40°18.614' W105°38.724'

9 Cub Lake Trailhead: *Cub Lake*

SCENERY: ✿ ✿ ✿ ✿   CHILDREN: ✿ ✿ ✿ ✿

DIFFICULTY: ✿ ✿   SOLITUDE: ✿ ✿

TRAIL CONDITION: ✿ ✿ ✿ ✿   HIKING TIME: 2½ hours

DISTANCE: 4.6 miles out-and-back

FLOOD IMPACT: 0

OUTSTANDING FEATURES: Moraine Park, wildlife, wildflowers, birds, alpine lake

---

JUST LIKE THE SONG, this hike goes over the river and through the woods, with a meadow and some elk thrown in. Kids will love this hike, as will those new to hiking, and also experienced hikers who want to slow down and appreciate the view. Cub Lake is a popular hike, so I recommend that you hike during the week and in shoulder seasons.

🚶🚶   Leave the trailhead and cross the bridge. Pass the sign for Cub Lake that says your destination is in 2.4 miles. (The Pool is 3.5 miles; Mill Creek Basin is 4 miles away). The path is doubletrack and sandy. There is enough room for hikers to walk side by side. Cross another bridge that passes over the Big Thompson River. To the left is the grassy and wildflower-filled meadow of the Moraine Park valley. To the immediate right is a forest full of pine trees. Views of Stones Peak, Sprague Mountain, and Gabletop Mountain can be seen from the bridge.

The trail travels up and down at a steady pace, but continues alongside the meadow of Moraine Park. You'll have the meadow views until the path goes around a large boulder on man-made stairs, making a sharp turn, thus interrupting the level journey across Moraine Park. Hikers soon travel away from Moraine Park and join up with Cub Creek, heading west.

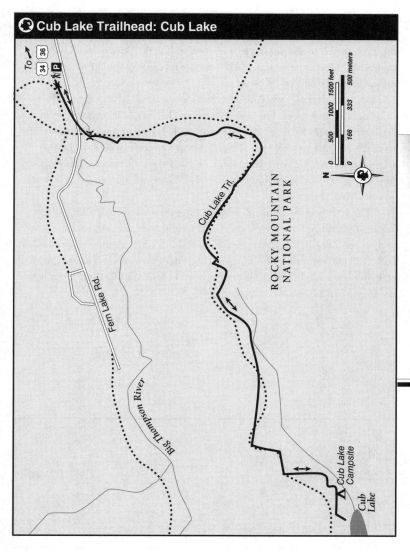

Cub Lake Trailhead: Cub Lake

To
34 36
N P

500 1000 1500 feet
0 166 333 500 meters

N

ROCKY MOUNTAIN
NATIONAL PARK

Cub Lake Trl.

Fern Lake Rd.

Big Thompson River

Cub Lake
Campsite

Cub
Lake

At the first fork in the trail, turn right toward Cub Lake. The trail is now singletrack, soft, and sandy, and travels at a mild ascent. Hike toward the mountains and continue west past the wetlands area. Here you will likely see plenty of ducks in the summer. Elk are notorious for populating this area, especially Moraine Park, all year.

At times, light scrambling over rocks is required. The trail continues to be narrow and rocky, but generally level. The path is shaded with a lot of ferns and foliage that hug the side of the trail. March onward, but take time to enjoy the journey. We were cruising by on a summer weekday when we came across a couple from Boulder, originally from Germany. The man saw us rushing and said something profound: "When you stop and sit a minute, you really see things."

The trail begins to ascend through aspen trees and rock piles. As you begin to see more flora and fauna, the trail becomes rockier and little streams pepper the sides. Once we decided to slow down a bit, we did see more. One such find was a number of mountain chickadees that were peeping around the trail. We saw a single chickadee pop its head in and out of a nest, from inside the hole of an aspen tree.

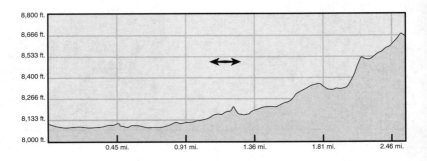

The trail switches back two or three times and starts to steepen. (My hiking partner called it an "abrupt change of personality.") Pass the intersection of Cub Lake Trail with the Cub Creek Campsite. Continue straight. Pass another sign pointing to the Cub Creek Privy. The final destination is Cub Lake. As the name implies, it's a cute little place—not too imposing, but substantial in its own right—with big lily pads, marshy shores, and surrounded on all sides by grass and pine trees. Mountain peaks in view are Stones Peak and Sprague Mountain.

The wildlife at the lake is quite tame, but beware of the ducks and chipmunks when you bring out your food. When we stopped, a ravenous duck attacked our picnic.

DIRECTIONS From Rocky Mountain National Park's Beaver Meadows Entrance, take Bear Lake Road south for 1.2 miles, and then turn right toward the Moraine Park Campground. After 0.7 mile, turn left and follow the signs to Cub Lake.

GPS TRAILHEAD COORDINATES
N40°21.327' W105°36.699'

10 Deer Ridge Junction Trailhead:
Deer Mountain

SCENERY: ✿ ✿ ✿ ✿

DIFFICULTY: ✿ ✿ ✿ ✿

TRAIL CONDITION: ✿ ✿ ✿ ✿

DISTANCE: 6 miles out-and-back

FLOOD IMPACT: **0**

CHILDREN: ✿ ✿

SOLITUDE: ✿ ✿ ✿

HIKING TIME: 3½ hours

OUTSTANDING FEATURES: Meadows, aspen groves, summit views:
Ypsilon Mountain, Longs Peak, Estes Park

DEER MOUNTAIN IS GREAT for people who want a short but strenuous hike with beautiful rewards—the views! Consider this a conditioning hike, or a first summit hike for newbies. An early start on a weekday will help avoid the crowds, horses, heat, and afternoon summer thunderstorms.

Leave the trailhead and head through the scattered ponderosa pine trees and rock outcroppings. The trail is sandy, and there is very little foliage surrounding the edges. Along with the spaciousness at the beginning of the trail comes exposure to the sun. The sun blazes on this first mile, so be sure to have plenty of water. Look to the northwest for the first views of Ypsilon Mountain. Its Y-shaped gash on the face makes it easy to recognize.

Take a right at the intersection of Aspen Glen Campground and Deer Mountain Summit, heading toward Deer Mountain. Before the 1-mile point, look downhill toward Beaver Meadows and the views of Longs Peak in the background. A gorgeous aspen grove marches up and down the hill, rounding out a perfect scene.

The forest now offers a respite in the form of shade—but not for long. A single switchback sends hikers back across the exposed slope, along the

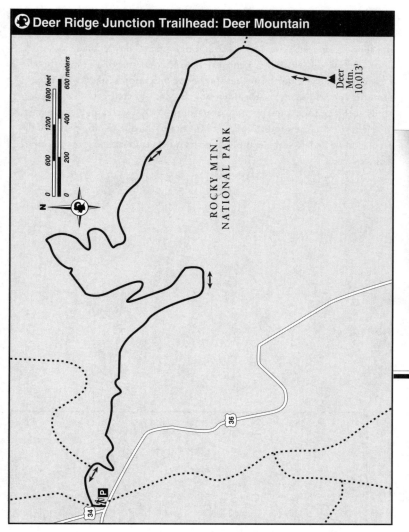

Deer Ridge Junction Trailhead: Deer Mountain

Deer Mtn. 10,013'

ROCKY MTN. NATIONAL PARK

N

1800 feet
1200
600
0

600 meters
400
200
0

36

34

N P

GORGE LAKES AREA
AND BEAR LAKE AREA

mountainside, traveling at a steep sideways angle as it traverses. The shade reappears, as does a small descent. Don't get too excited because this is what you'll be dealing with for the next two hours: up and down, shade and then no shade, switchback after switchback—the roller coaster of a summit hike.

The trail levels out 1 mile before the top and tempts hikers with false summits and confusing, sandy side trails. Stay on the main trail (it's also sandy at this point), and continue onward until you reach a sign that marks the right turn to the summit of Deer Mountain. This 0.2-mile path is well earned and a relief, as the summit appears quickly after a short march up a stone stairway.

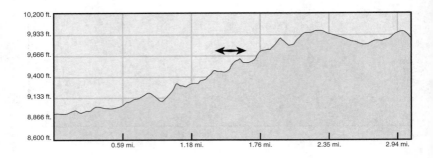

The Deer Mountain summit is characterized by flat-topped boulders, snaggled trees, and views in all directions. At nearly 10,000 feet, hikers will either be greeted by peace and sunshine, or wicked weather with whipping winds and lightning. Plan accordingly, because either scenario can happen, and the weather could change quickly. Rest here and turn around, heading the way that you came.

DIRECTIONS   From Rocky Mountain National Park's Beaver Meadows Entrance, take US 36 west to the intersection of US 36 and US 34. Deer Ridge Junction is on the right, before the roads meet. Park in the pulloffs along the shoulder.

GPS TRAILHEAD COORDINATES
N40°23.107' W105°36.579'

East Portal Trailhead:
Wind River and Glacier Basin Loop

SCENERY: ☆ ☆ ☆

DIFFICULTY: ☆ ☆ ☆

TRAIL CONDITION: ☆ ☆ ☆ ☆

DISTANCE: 5.06 miles, loop

FLOOD IMPACT: **0**

OUTSTANDING FEATURES: River

CHILDREN: ☆ ☆ ☆

SOLITUDE: ☆ ☆ ☆

HIKING TIME: 2½ hours

THE EAST PORTAL TRAILHEAD, which is run by Larimer County Parks and Recreation, is a nice park secret. From here, you can access Glacier Basin, the Glacier Creek Trail, the Storm Pass Trail, the Wind River Trail, Emerald Mountain, and two unofficial summits. The loop featured here is a great hike to do if you want to be close to the town of Estes Park but away from the crowds.

The trailhead is part of the Alva B. Adams Tunnel property. Part of the Colorado–Big Thompson project, it's one of the main tunnels bringing water from Lake Granby and Shadow Mountain Lake on the west side to the Front Range and the plains. Water exits here, goes down the Big Thompson River to Estes Park and through several power plants, all the way down to the lower elevations. The tunnel is 13.1 miles long.

Proceed from the parking area, which holds about 10 cars, on Wind River Trail. You'll cross a small, open area with signs notifying you that you are on US government property, but not in Rocky Mountain National Park. The Department of Reclamation maintains the tunnels and owns the land, so the trail signs are not as friendly as those in Rocky Mountain National Park. This trail is also not as well marked as those in Rocky Mountain National Park.

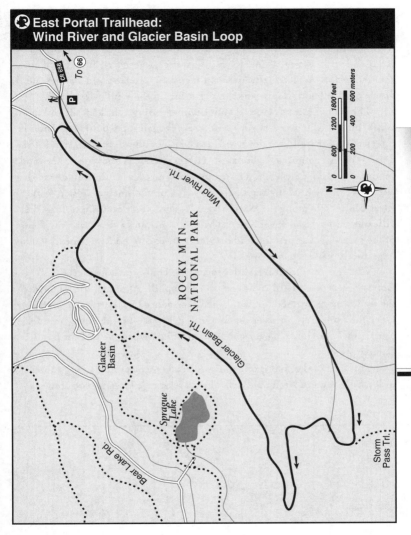

East Portal Trailhead:
Wind River and Glacier Basin Loop

CR 69B
To 66
P
N

1800 feet
1200
600
600 meters
400
200
0
0

N

GORGE LAKES AREA
AND BEAR LAKE AREA

Wind River Trl.

ROCKY MTN.
NATIONAL PARK

Glacier Basin Trl.

Glacier Basin

Sprague Lake

Bear Lake Rd.

Storm Pass Trl.

A steady incline brings hikers through sage brush, scattered ponderosa pines, and junipers. Minutes into the hike, pass a sign that says Entering Rocky Mountain National Park. Continue up about another 100 yards on a sandy and rocky ascent. Come to an intersection where a right turn will take you to the YMCA, and a left, up the hill, goes to Glacier Basin Campground. Take a hard left and traverse the slope, staying on the Wind River Trail.

The trail continues to wind and meander, going a little bit up and then a little bit down. It gets very rocky and goes through some boulders. Another intersection is a trail back down to East Portal Trailhead. Stay on Wind River Trail, veering right on a slight ascent. Hikers enter a shadier forest here and get out of the sun a little bit. The Wind River cascades off the boulder to the left. Pass a horse hitching rail where there is a single, small campsite, Wind River Bluff, right along the Wind River. Pass two more campsites: Over the Hill and Upper Wind River Site 1. The trail continues a steady ascent. Views of the ridges above open up, and on your left, pass Wind River Site 2. Pass a large and very old aspen grove.

The next intersection is with Storm Pass Trail, which leads to Estes Cone. Hikers take a hard right and proceed uphill. Although still wooded, the trail is more exposed to the weather as evidenced by the gnarled trees. Once the trail levels off, keep an eye out for the easy-to-miss turn onto Glacier Basin Trail. Take a hard right here, heading toward the Glacier Basin Campground.

This part of the trail is one of the official cross-country skiing routes in Rocky Mountain National Park. There are orange blaze tags on some of

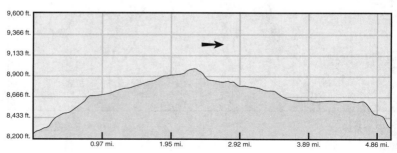

the trees to help you find the routes during winter. It's relatively easy to hike here, and this area is popular, especially among people coming from Bear Lake Road. Continue straight as you pass an intersection with the trail to the left, heading toward Sprague Lake and the more popular trails near Bear Lake Road. Pass another intersection, where a left turn will also take you back toward the Bear Lake Road trails.

You'll see a maintenance road to your left; it leads to a park-service campground. Continue along, passing a huge metal water tank. Take a right at the intersection with the YMCA Trail, and go uphill. This is a trail used mainly by the YMCA for its horses. You'll have views of the perfectly conical mountain that is Estes Cone. A quick descent through an aspen grove will take hikers across an open sagebrush-covered slope. Resist the temptation to take a shortcut downhill and go another quarter mile back to the trailhead.

DIRECTIONS From Estes Park, take US 36 toward Rocky Mountain National Park. Take the first left after Marys Lake Road onto CO 66. Follow the signs to the YMCA. This road becomes County Road 69B. Pass the YMCA and go another mile until the road ends. There is a small day-use parking area about 100 yards before the road ends; park here.

GPS TRAILHEAD COORDINATES
N40°19.553' W105°34.684'

12 Fern Lake Trailhead:
Fern Lake and Old Forest Inn Campsite

SCENERY: ☆ ☆ ☆ ☆ ☆

DIFFICULTY: ☆ ☆ ☆ ☆
(to campsite ☆ ☆)

TRAIL CONDITION: ☆ ☆ ☆ ☆

CHILDREN: ☆ ☆
(to campsite ☆ ☆ ☆ ☆)

SOLITUDE: ☆ ☆ ☆

HIKING TIME: 4½ hours
(1½ hours to campsite)

DISTANCE: 7.6 miles (2.89 miles to campsite)

FLOOD IMPACT: ☆ The trail beyond Fern Lake is not featured here, but you will encounter significant damage if you continue. On Odessa Lake Trail the trail edge is missing along Fern Creek, and the bridge is missing across Fern Creek to Odessa Lake.

OUTSTANDING FEATURES: Two waterfalls, alpine lake, The Pool, Arch Rocks, Big Thompson River, Old Forest Inn history

THE OLD FOREST INN CAMPSITE is the best backcountry site for first-time campers. It's in proximity to Bear Lake access, without the Bear Lake crowds. The beauty of the campsites here attests to the perfect location of an old inn that no longer exists. This hike also offers plenty of easy yet scenic miles, and even more miles of leg-burning uphill. The ascents are rewarded, of course, with the amazing water shows of Marguerite Falls and Fern Falls, as well as Fern Lake. Take the whole family on this outing, camp, and then split up according to fitness level when you're ready to explore.

🏃 Leave the trailhead and travel through a forest canopy of various aspen and pine trees. The trail is level for the first mile and very damp, which is uncharacteristic of the Rocky Mountain region. A wide variety of wet, moisture-rich plants live along the banks of the nearby Big Thompson River. Along with the pine and aspen trees, there is a huge variety of trees such as mountain maple trees and river birch trees. Then there are the ferns that carpet the forest ground, thus giving the hike, lake, and falls their namesake.

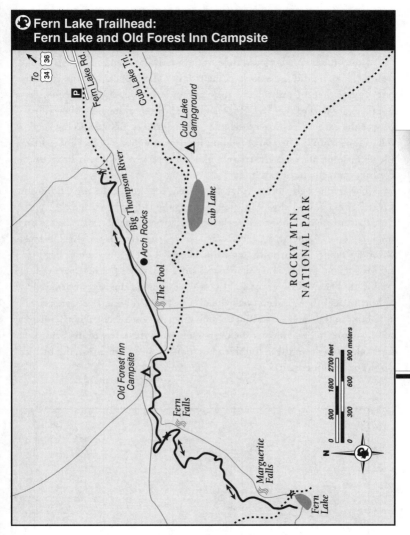

Fern Lake Trailhead:
Fern Lake and Old Forest Inn Campsite

To 34 36

Fern Lake Rd.

P

Cub Lake Trl.

Cub Lake Campground

Big Thompson River

Arch Rocks

The Pool

Cub Lake

ROCKY MTN. NATIONAL PARK

Old Forest Inn Campsite

Fern Falls

Marguerite Falls

Fern Lake

N

900 1800 2700 feet
0
0 300 600 900 meters

GORGE LAKES AREA
AND BEAR LAKE AREA

The trail is singletrack packed dirt. Pass by the river on the left and then pass through an old rockslide. The trail is still level, and any type of incline hikers encounter early on is aided by man-made, rock staircases.

Continue through a giant field of boulders that might make you stop to wonder, "Where did these rocks come from?" They appear so random and out of place that the only logical answer is outer space. All joking aside, these boulders are part of the Arch Rocks, and according to the park, they were part of the early formation of the park, when glaciers melted and big rocks fell to the ground. The giant, red boulders tower almost 30 feet above hikers, tilting in some places to create arch-like bridges above. There is also a back-country campsite in this vicinity.

The trail travels along a ridge after Arch Rocks, with the Big Thompson River flowing down below. Go straight along the ridge for a while.

Pass through another old rockslide and various social trails, staying on the main trail. Come to a large wooden bridge that crosses the Big Thompson River and, more importantly, signifies The Pool. This is a popular destination for school groups and other hikers since it's only 1.5 miles from the trailhead. The Pool is part of an expansive cascade on the river, bordered by a short rock cliff. Although every time I have traveled here, I've seen hikers splashing in the water or sliding on embankments or hillsides, it's best to stay on the main trail and look at the deep water from the safety of the bridge. One false step down there could lead to disaster, not to mention the impact on the environment.

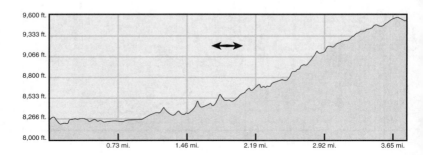

Set up camp at the Old Forest Inn Campsite, stretch your legs, and head up, up, up to Fern Falls (pictured on page 78), Marguerite Falls, and Fern Lake pictured here.

Cross the bridge at The Pool and take a sharp right toward Fern Lake. Head up into the rocks where you will see a sign that says Fern Odessa. (Fern Lake and Odessa Lake are both lake destinations on this trail.) Cross over the bridge and then arrive at the turn for the Old Forest Inn Campsite.

Overnight Option: Take a right and follow the red arrowheads on the trees. There are two sites. The site to the left, or the north, is our favorite because it offers views similar to the ones travelers would have had at the Old Forest Inn. It also has an amazing view of the Big Thompson River below, as well as a gentle river sound, and flat boulders good for camp housekeeping. There are a maximum of two tents at the north site. Higher up on the hill, to the right after turning off the trail, is another campsite that sits above The Pool. This site is a little more exposed, but both sites are in a stand of spruce

77

and fir trees. These sites are attractive because they're easy to get to, but once you get off the trail and up the hill a little bit, all the people disappear.

The Forest Inn was a summer hotel and resort that operated in one form or another until 1949. According to the *Estes Park Trail Gazette,* the buildings were torn down in the spring of 1959 and a calendar found at the site before the demolition was dated 1952. It's interesting to note that there are many lost lodges in Rocky Mountain National Park, including Fern Lodge at Fern Lake, your end hiking destination. Most of these lost lodges were purchased and removed by the park, albeit with much controversy.

A thundering Fern Falls—somewhere to revisit again and again, as it is always changing.

Back on Track: After setting up camp or spending the night, the more experienced of your group will continue to Fern Lake. It should be stressed that the ease of the first portion of the trail is by no means representative of the trek to Fern Lake. Let the little ones and the tired ones play, explore, or make lunch around the campsite.

The trail is level and travels along small falls and crosses a split-log bridge. To the left is Fern Falls, and then the real climbing begins. As you approach her, you can hear the sounds of Marguerite Falls. This magnificent water show is worth the effort and a good place to stop and rest. Take the large switchback up the hill after the falls and continue to climb. There is no respite until you get to where the trail intersects with the turn for Spruce Lake and the backcountry campsites for Fern Lake. Continue over the hill to Fern Lake. An old patrol cabin sits to the right. Once you reach the alpine shore of Fern Lake you see Notchtop Mountain and Little Matterhorn rising above the other side of the lake.

After a rest, go back the way you came—downhill this time—to your campsite or the trailhead. On your return, be sure to encourage all the hikers who will undoubtedly ask you "How much farther?" The mileage from Fern Falls to Fern Lake is 1 mile. However, the ascent makes it feel farther because hikers are traveling at less than 1.5 miles per hour.

DIRECTIONS   From the Beaver Meadows Entrance, take Bear Lake Road south for 1.2 miles, and turn right toward Moraine Park Campground. After 0.7 mile, turn left and follow the signs to Cub Lake and Fern Lake. Continue to the Fern Lake Trailhead road and take a left. Travel to the very end of this road and park at the trailhead, an obvious dead end. In the winter, this 0.7-mile stretch is usually closed, so you will have to park at the turnoff where you see the restrooms and a large parking area.

GPS TRAILHEAD COORDINATES
N40°21.091' W105°38.315'

13 Hermit Park: *Kruger Rock Trail*

SCENERY: ✿ ✿ ✿ ✿　　　　CHILDREN: ✿ ✿ ✿

DIFFICULTY: ✿ ✿ ✿　　　　SOLITUDE: ✿ ✿ ✿ ✿

TRAIL CONDITION: ✿ ✿ ✿　　HIKING TIME: 2½ hours

DISTANCE: 3.6 miles, out-and-back

FLOOD IMPACT: 0

OUTSTANDING FEATURES: Meadow, forest, views of Estes Park, Rocky Mountain National Park, Mount Meeker, Longs Peak, Continental Divide, and Mummy Range

KRUGER ROCK TRAIL IS LOCATED in Larimer County's Hermit Park Open Space. The historic Hermit Park is a relatively new park (it opened in 2008) approximately 2 miles southeast of Estes Park. This hike is easy to find and makes for a great workout, with an elevation gain of more than 900 feet. Much of the trail offers a rarely seen perspective of Rocky Mountain National Park, and the views are worth the trip alone.

🚶🚶 Pass through the parking lot and head toward the pavilion, picnic tables, restrooms, and horseshoe pits. Cross through the trees via a short path. Protected wetlands and fields surround the trailhead area on either side.

Cross the main road and travel to the main Kruger Rock Trailhead. The trail climbs gradually up an open hillside and passes through a small meadow dotted with wildflowers in the summer. Fireweed, Indian paintbrush, and aspen trees are plentiful. Continue in this direction at a slight incline. The aspen trees become dense as you pass a large rock outcropping to the left of the trail.

Turning to the north, you will come to the first switchback of the trail. The switchback takes you through a boulder field where the first elevated views of the Rocky Mountain National Park and Lake Estes can be seen. The

Hermit Park: Kruger Rock Trail

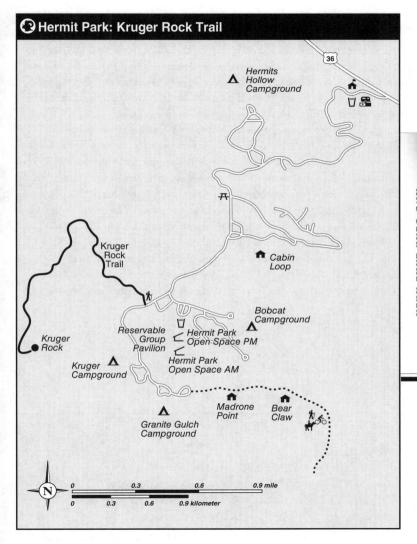

switchbacks continue to ease the climb, and what comes up does come down, at least a little bit here and there, so expect some respite.

The first such break comes with a slight decline in the trail as it leads to a false summit where the first views of the Mummy Range can be seen to the northwest. A short descent follows the ridge to the southwest, keeping the Mummy Range in view. The trail becomes sandy in small patches during the slight decent, with rocky outcroppings popping up throughout.

The trail eventually crosses the ridge, temporarily hiding the views of Mummy Range. Don't fret as the trail then crosses over the ridge again, keeping with the ascent, and bringing the mountain range back into scope. The trail continues slightly downward until it reaches another false summit that offers a 180-degree view of the park and the surrounding mountains. At this point the trail begins a steep climb as it switchbacks up the ascent. The trail will eventually flatten out ever so slightly as it leads southwest along the mountain. You'll have views of Longs Peak, Mount Meeker, and the Continental Divide.

The switchbacks continue up the mountain, and your destination, Kruger Rock, comes into full view; however, another false summit dashes those dreams of glory. At this point there are two options: Turn around and

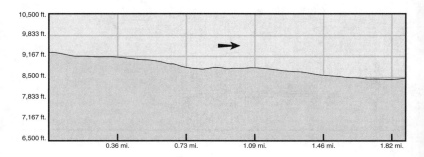

head back the way you came, or put your game face on and make the trek up Kruger Rock. Routes through the middle or around the west side of Kruger Rock require some scrambling.

When you're finished, turn around and head down the trail back to the parking lot.

TAKE NOTE

Dogs are allowed and must be leashed. The cabins here are really cute, and the tent campsites are top-notch. Stick around Hermit Park (**larimer.org /naturalresources**) if you want to try some of the other new trails or if you want to check out the cabins for a return overnight visit. You may reserve campsites or cabins by visiting **larimercamping.com** or calling 800-397-7795.

DIRECTIONS   From Denver, take I-25 north to CO 66 and travel west on CO 66 for 16 miles to Lyons. Turn right onto West Main Street onto CO 36 west. Continue on CO 36 for 16.7 miles. The entrance to Hermit Park is on the left. Pay the $6 daily entrance fee per vehicle. Take the dirt road to the Kruger Rock Trail parking area near the Pavilion.

GPS TRAILHEAD COORDINATES
N40°20.195' W105°29.108'

14 Hollowell Park Trailhead:
Mill Creek Balloon

SCENERY: ✪ ✪ ✪ ✪

DIFFICULTY: ✪ ✪

TRAIL CONDITION: ✪ ✪ ✪

DISTANCE: 3.4 miles out-and-back

FLOOD IMPACT: **0**

CHILDREN: ✪ ✪ ✪ ✪

SOLITUDE: ✪ ✪ ✪

HIKING TIME: 1¾ hours

OUTSTANDING FEATURES: Meadow, aspen trees, views, loop hike, stream, beaver dams

---

LOOP HIKES IN ROCKY MOUNTAIN NATIONAL PARK are rare, so this small balloon hike is a nice change of pace. The fall colors along the Mill Creek Basin are striking because of the patches of aspens that make their home here. Novice hikers will appreciate the scenery and the ease of this trail. Seasoned hikers like this trail for its access to other areas of the park, its beauty, and the surprising lack of crowds despite proximity to the park entrance.

🧍🧍 Leave the trailhead and enter into the meadow where dry grasses are framed by views of the surrounding moraines. The trail is sandy and dusty, yet smooth and level. If there is no rain, hikers will kick up a lot of dust onto their hiking boots in this section.

Look for the strip of aspen trees on Bierstadt Moraine that is especially striking in September, when the aspen leaves turn golden. The light-colored trees growing on the forest's slope are aspens that mark an old logging skid trial. Lumbermen hauled timbers from the saw mill up near Bierstadt Lake to build the Stanley Hotel.

The trail is still on level ground as it continues to pass through the silver and green sagebrush that lines the path. Pine trees begin to close in on the

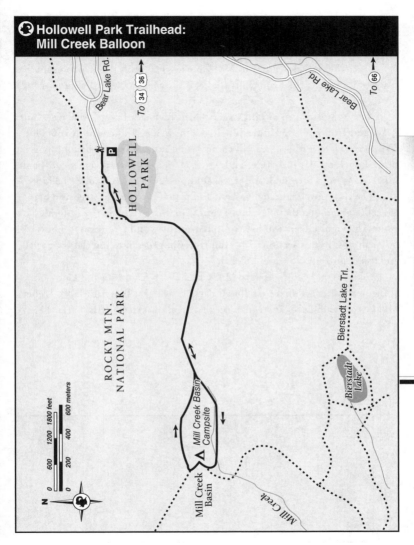

Hollowell Park Trailhead:
Mill Creek Balloon

Bear Lake Rd.

To 34 36

Bear Lake Rd.

To 66

P

HOLLOWELL PARK

GORGE LAKES AREA
AND BEAR LAKE AREA

ROCKY MTN.
NATIONAL PARK

Bierstadt Lake Trl.

Bierstadt Lake

Mill Creek Basin Campsite

Mill Creek Basin

Mill Creek

0   600   1200   1800 feet
0   200   400   600 meters

N

trail, although there are still views of Longs Peak to the left. Continue straight at the intersection of Hollowell Park Trail, Mill Creek Basin, and the horse trail to Moraine Park, which makes a sharp right behind you.

Once the trail gets closer to Mill Creek, social trails travel away from the main trail. Stay on the main trail as it begins to make a gradual climb through the trees.

At the intersection of Mill Creek Basin, Bierstadt Lake, Bear Lake, Cub Lake, and Hollowell Park, turn left across the bridge and continue on. The trail to the right is where you will come down, completing the balloon portion of the loop. (If you prefer an intense elevation gain and a more difficult hike, take a right turn here and travel counterclockwise around the balloon.)

The trail travels at a slight ascent and is full of rocks. The erosion here is a telltale sign that there is a lot of runoff in this area when the rainwater comes through. Hikers will have to step over rocks and tree roots, among other things, in this section. The trail rolls on, gets sandy and flat for a spell, and then continues to travel upward.

Take a right heading toward Mill Creek Basin Campsite and Cub Lake at the next junction where Hollowell Park, Bear Lake, Bierstadt Lake, Upper Mill Creek, Cub Lake, and Mill Creek Basin all intersect. This marks the

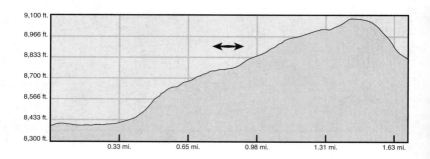

1.7-mile point. Mill Creek Basin is a meadow framed by Mount Wuh to the west and Steep Mountain to the northeast. When you get to the next intersection, take a right and head in a clockwise pattern back to the main trail. Cross over the creek via a bridge and pass a horse hitch on the right.

The trail travels through short meadows and trees now. Take a sharp right and continue to Hollowell Park at the intersection of Hollowell Park, Cub Lake, and Mill Creek Basin Campsite. The trail ascends one more time, levels out, and drops us back down to where we came from. The trail descends sharply, is very steep, and not in the best condition. What is striking is how the aspen trees frame the trail—they look like they are standing in wait as you head downward. The aspen trees through here are uncharacteristically big and old. Eventually you reach the forest floor and get to walk alongside the trees. Then you will meet up with the main trail where you head straight back to the trailhead by retracing your steps.

DIRECTIONS   From the Beaver Meadows Entrance, take Bear Lake Road south for 3.5 miles. Turn right at the Hollowell Park Trailhead. Drive a few hundred yards to the parking area.

GPS TRAILHEAD COORDINATES
N40°20.379' W105°36.274'

15 Upper Beaver Meadows Trailhead: *Ute Meadows Loop*

SCENERY: ☆ ☆ ☆ ☆

DIFFICULTY: ☆ ☆ ☆ ☆

TRAIL CONDITION: ☆ ☆ ☆

DISTANCE: 8.5 miles out-and-back

FLOOD IMPACT: 0

CHILDREN: ☆ ☆

SOLITUDE: ☆ ☆ ☆

HIKING TIME: 5 hours

OUTSTANDING FEATURES: Meadow, forest, wildlife, stream, views of Longs Peak and Deer Mountain

THE UPPER BEAVER MEADOWS LOOP is a nice hike in its own right, but the spur trail to the Ute Meadows Campsite makes it even more interesting. The Beaver Meadows portion is mostly arid, with sweeping views of the heart of Rocky Mountain National Park. The trek to the Ute Meadows Campsite is an uphill hike and quite a challenge with backpacking gear. The campsite is llama accessible, so this may be your chance to get some help packing it in.

🏃 Leave the trailhead and follow the signs to the Ute Meadows Campsite, staying on the right-hand trail when the path makes its immediate split. This is the intersection of Beaver Meadows Trailhead, Moraine Park, Ute Meadows Campsite, and Trail Ridge Road. The trails seem to meander in and out at this point, so it is important to remember to stay in a direction that heads toward the Ute Trail.

The trail starts out wide and sandy before turning into a singletrack, ascending at a gentle grade as the views of Moraine Valley to the left gradually begin to disappear. Start to travel through the forest. After 1.5 miles, reach the junction of Beaver Meadows Trailhead, Ute Meadows Campsite, and Trail

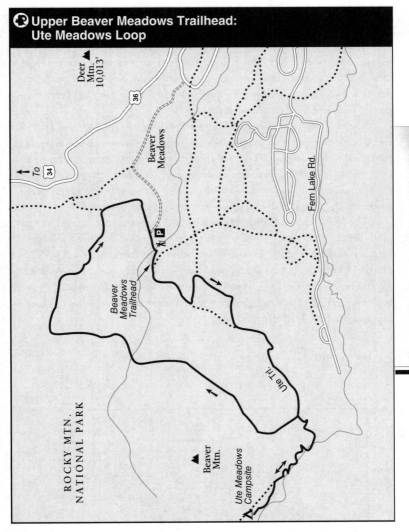

Upper Beaver Meadows Trailhead: Ute Meadows Loop

Deer Mtn. 10,013'

36

To 34

Beaver Meadows

Fern Lake Rd.

P

Beaver Meadows Trailhead

ROCKY MTN. NATIONAL PARK

Ute Trl.

Beaver Mtn.

Ute Meadows Campsite

Ridge Road. It is now another 1.2 miles to the campsite. Take the left trail heading forward on the Ute Trail.

The views to the left now open up to Longs Peak and Mount Meeker as the path enters the Windy Gulch area. The trail has a very steep ascent right after the intersection. Don't forget to look out at the views as you catch your breath. As you gain elevation, the views below are of the Cub Lake area. The path is faint and hard to follow in spots.

The trail then opens up, looking west to the timberline area of Trail Ridge. Hikers might have to scramble over some rocks here. Keep an eye out for cairns to stay on track. The trail then makes a quick descent and travels along a small, shady stream. The next intersection is an indicator for Beaver Mountain Trailhead, 2.8 miles (this is how far we have come), and Trail Ridge Road, 3.8 miles. Here, take a left turn into the campsite.

The Ute Meadows Campsite is a beautiful camping spot located in a dry, sandy area. You'll cross a small stream to get to the site; the forest will be to your left and the meadow to your right, behind the trees. After a night's rest, turn back onto the Ute Trail and head back the way that you came. Wondering where the Ute Trail goes if you continue in the other direction? It travels over Timberline Pass, through Tombstone Ridge, and ends at the Ute Crossing Trailhead on Trail Ridge Road.

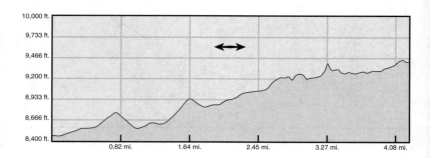

This hiker minds her step on an arid portion of the Upper Beaver Meadows loop hike.

After backtracking, arrive at the junction of the Ute Trail and Upper Beaver Meadows. Turn left to begin a clockwise loop around Upper Beaver Meadows; it's 3.5 miles to the Upper Beaver Meadows Trailhead. The trail travels at a slow but pleasant ascent, and there are views to the right of Longs Peak. Soon the sun will hit the trail as it winds through small, forested pockets and continues onward.

Park views from the Upper Beaver Meadows hike—a nice respite in the shade of the trees.

Cross two streams and then travel down into a meadow. The trail here is sandy, and it begins another moderate climb through the forest. You can now see Trail Ridge Road in some spots and the first sightings of Deer Mountain. The trail is very exposed in the open meadow as you pass the intersection with Deer Ridge Junction. Stay on the main trail and travel back to the Upper Beaver Meadows Trailhead in a descent through the meadow. The trail ends on the access road, and you must walk the last 50 feet on the pavement back to your car.

DIRECTIONS From the Beaver Meadows Entrance, take US 36 west to the turnoff for the Upper Beaver Meadows Trailhead, just before the junction with US 34. Turn left onto the dirt road and drive 2 miles until it ends at the parking lot and trailhead.

GPS TRAILHEAD COORDINATES
N40°22.274' W105°36.799'

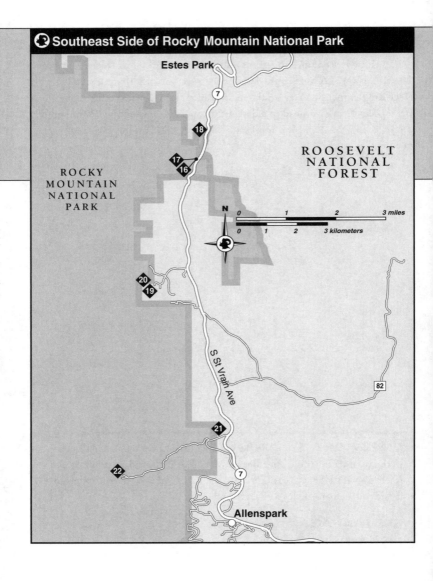

Estes Park

ROOSEVELT
NATIONAL
FOREST

ROCKY
MOUNTAIN
NATIONAL
PARK

N

0   1   2   3 miles

0   1   2   3 kilometers

S St Vrain Ave

82

7

Allenspark

SOUTHEAST SIDE
OF ROCKY MOUNTAIN
NATIONAL PARK
(Longs Peak Area and Wild Basin Area)

HIKE 19 *Longs Peak (see page 109). It's always best to start this hike early, as the sun begins to rise. An early start helps with crowds and the always-changing weather.*

16 Lily Lake Trailhead: *Lily Ridge Trail*

SCENERY: ✰ ✰ ✰ ✰   CHILDREN: ✰ ✰ ✰ ✰ ✰

DIFFICULTY: ✰   SOLITUDE: ✰ ✰

TRAIL CONDITION: ✰ ✰ ✰ ✰   HIKING TIME: 45 minutes

DISTANCE: 1.34 miles, loop

FLOOD IMPACT: 0

OUTSTANDING FEATURES: Lake, views

LILY RIDGE TRAIL OFFERS SOMETHING for everyone. This hike around Lily Lake gives beginners their first experience with an ascent and gets kids out of the stroller and onto the trail. This is a popular spot for anglers, picnickers, and hikers. Anglers line the shore and can be found bobbing around in individual fishing tubes.

🚶🚶   The trailhead and parking area for Lily Lake are across the road from Lily Lake Visitor Center, which is currently closed. Leave the trailhead; turn right onto the trail directly along the perimeter of the lake. Take a right turn before the wooden bridge at the sign that says LILY RIDGE TRAIL. Start heading upward at a gradual ascent. Continue on gentle switchbacks and scramble over the rock steps in the path.

The Lily Ridge Trail travels from the east end of Lily Lake to its west end along the ridge to the north of the lake. Immediately look out across Lily Lake toward Longs Peak. Begin to head away from the views of the lake and up over a fake summit and ridge. Now you will glance toward Estes Park and see the rooftops of Camp Cheley.

The trail levels off and heads west along the ridge a few hundred feet above the lake. Cross up through large rocks to a small bench that offers a

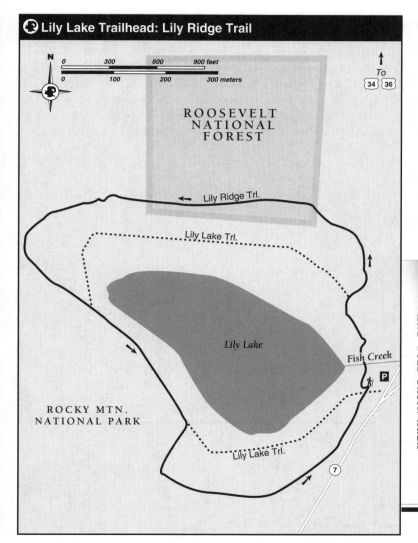

Lily Lake Trailhead: Lily Ridge Trail

N

0   300   600   900 feet
0   100   200   300 meters

To
34 36

ROOSEVELT
NATIONAL
FOREST

← Lily Ridge Trl.

Lily Lake Trl.

Lily Lake

Fish Creek

P

ROCKY MTN.
NATIONAL PARK

Lily Lake Trl.

7

LONGS PEAK AREA
AND WILD BASIN AREA

nice respite and fantastic views of Longs Peak. Continue along the counter-clockwise loop on the ridge along the trail.

Descent begins around the back side of the lake, on the west end. The descent is gradual and easy on the legs, heading back to the shores of Lily Lake. This lake is the beginning of Fish Creek, which flows into Lake Estes. The Lily Lake Trail is wheelchair accessible, wide, level, and lined by logs.

Pass the intersection of Lily Ridge Trail and Lily Lake Trail. Continue straight, and then take a left to stay on Lily Lake Trail. The Lily Ridge Trail is

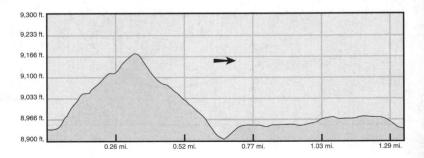

complete at this point. Do not go right onto the service road. From this vantage point you can see the Twin Sisters Peaks toward the east.

At the next trail intersection, take the right-hand spur trail that heads south to more shade and nice picnic spots with tables. Keep following this trail until you return back to the parking area and trailhead.

DIRECTIONS From Estes Park, go south on CO 7, past Marys Lake. The road curves sharply and travels to Lily Lake Visitor Center on the left. Turn right here and park in the small lot across the street and adjacent to the lake.

GPS TRAILHEAD COORDINATES
N40°18.292' W105°32.234'

17 Lily Lake Trailhead: *Twin Sisters Peaks*

SCENERY: ✿ ✿ ✿

DIFFICULTY: ✿ ✿ ✿ ✿

TRAIL CONDITION: ✿ ✿ ✿

DISTANCE: 8 miles out-and-back

CHILDREN: ✿

SOLITUDE: ✿ ✿

HIKING TIME: 4 hours

FLOOD IMPACT: ✿ ✿ ✿ ✿ A massive landslide removed five switchbacks on the lower portion of the trail. Several alternative reroutes north of the landslide are under construction, as well as social trails that have developed. Restoration of this trail in its previous location may not be feasible. Twin Sisters Trail has evolved before, and trail segments abandoned due to reroutes are always restored to natural conditions.

OUTSTANDING FEATURES: Views of Estes Park, Rocky Mountain National Park; optimal views of Longs Peak; mostly shaded

THE TWIN SISTERS sit at the easternmost edge of Rocky Mountain National Park and are accessed without actually entering the park. The trail winds through forest with some of the best panoramic views of Longs Peak. This is a great conditioning climb for those wanting to tackle considerable elevations.

🏃 Start at Lily Lake Visitor Center. (The National Park Service abandoned the former Twin Sisters Trail, which began directly west of the summit in Tahosa Valley.) Park at the visitor center and hike the extra 0.3 mile to avoid the nightmare that is trying to park along the road, right before the true trailhead. Get on the road right behind the visitor center and follow it away from the highway. At the official trailhead for Twin Sisters, take a left onto the trail. Start out on a small service road bordered on both sides by a new evergreen-tree growth. Immediately on the left is a small wooden bridge, Twin Sisters Trail information, and a trail marker.

Start a steady ascent on a trail composed of loose rock and dirt. Enter a pine forest, and then enter U.S. Forest Service land as the trees crowd and

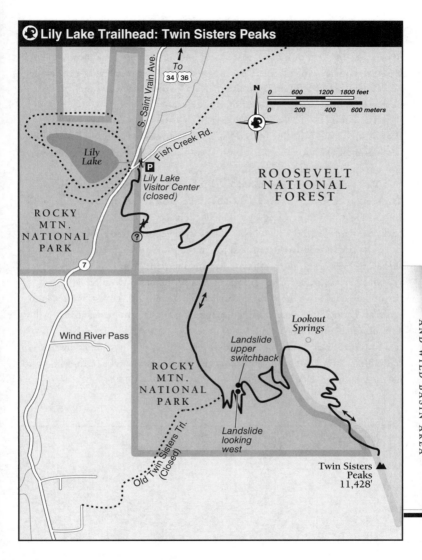

Lily Lake Trailhead: Twin Sisters Peaks

To
34 36

S. Saint Vrain Ave.

Fish Creek Rd.

Lily
Lake

Lily Lake
Visitor Center
(closed)

P

ROOSEVELT
NATIONAL
FOREST

N

0   600   1200   1800 feet
0   200   400   600 meters

ROCKY
MTN.
NATIONAL
PARK

7

Wind River Pass

Lookout
Springs

ROCKY
MTN.
NATIONAL
PARK

Landslide
upper
switchback

Landslide
looking
west

Old Twin Sisters Trl.
(Closed)

Twin Sisters
Peaks
11,428'

condense around the trail. Hikers ascend rather quickly and must scramble across some early rocks. The trail takes a deep right switchback and continues up the face of the mountain. Switchbacks and man-made rock staircases help lessen the burn of the ascent. Continue to climb, and then cross a rockslide and enter Rocky Mountain National Park. The trail becomes much steeper here, with a large staircase looming in the distance.

Turn and look to the right, taking in the first amazing views of Longs Peak as it rises up over the Tahosa Valley. Pass through a second rockslide and reach a small overlook. Continue as the trail starts a gradual descent, a welcome respite after all that uphill.

Pass a massive boulder and then climb a set of man-made rock stairs. The trail switches back again to the left and continues an uphill climb. You'll start to see aspen trees along with the tall, dense evergreens. Smaller switchbacks continue, and the trail is very rocky with exposed tree roots.

The trail continues its upward journey and then reaches an area where there are fewer trees, more shrubs, and small aspens. Here the trail is narrow and hard to navigate due to huge rocks in the path. Climb away from the hillside and leave the view of Longs Peak. Enter U.S. Forest Service land again and continue. After passing through the timberline, keep going to the summit area and head past the communications tower. The true Twin Sisters summit is not directly accessible by trail, but it can be reached by a brief scramble heading east from the communications tower. Take in the views and head back the way that you came.

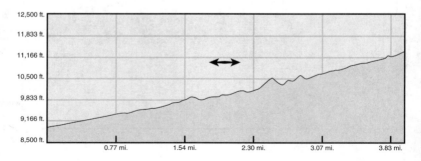

Views of Longs Peak are plentiful on Twin Sisters, but this little peek perfectly frames the peak. The mythical beaver climbing the side of the peak is expertly captured coming out of the trees to the left.

DIRECTIONS   From Estes Park, go south on CO 7, past Marys Lake. The road curves sharply and travels to Lily Lake Visitor Center on the left. Turn here and park.

GPS TRAILHEAD COORDINATES
N40°18.290' W105°32.167'

SCENERY: ✿ ✿ ✿

DIFFICULTY: ✿ ✿ ✿

TRAIL CONDITION: ✿ ✿ ✿ ✿

DISTANCE: 4 miles out-and-back

CHILDREN: ✿ ✿ ✿

SOLITUDE: ✿ ✿ ✿ ✿

HIKING TIME: 2½ hours

FLOOD IMPACT: **0** It is interesting to note that Aspen Brook Trail, which sits 0.5 mile from Lily Mountain, experienced severe flood damage. This trail accesses the historic Wigwam Tearoom; although it remains open, there is significant erosion and trenching that make Aspen Brook Trail one of the most flood-damaged trails.

OUTSTANDING FEATURES: Shaded alpine forest, views of Estes Park and Rocky Mountain National Park

---

LILY MOUNTAIN IS IDEAL for Estes Park visitors who don't have the time to hike into the heart of Rocky Mountain National Park. This is a classic alpine hike with rewarding views and a steady climb. Lily Mountain is often passed over for other hikes in the vicinity, such as Twin Sisters, and the hike is often confused with the small walk around Lily Lake. It's also often kept a secret and not listed in brochures, making this hike one of the least crowded around Estes Park.

🚶🚶 Leave the parking area and begin to climb directly from the trailhead. (There are no facilities here, only a call box. Parking is also very limited.) Pass a National Park Service boundary post and a Lily Mountain sign. The first half mile parallels CO 7 as the shaded trail begins its ascent along the ridge. Large pines and boulder clusters dominate the landscape here. The hard-packed dirt trail has loose rocks and some exposed tree roots. Expect snow on the trail if you hike outside of the recommended seasons. We hiked in early winter and encountered packed snow from the trailhead on.

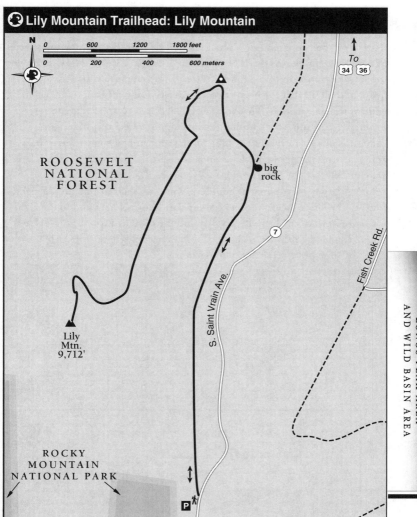

Lily Mountain Trailhead: Lily Mountain

N

0   600   1200   1800 feet
0   200   400   600 meters

ROOSEVELT
NATIONAL
FOREST

To
34 36

big
rock

7

Fish Creek Rd.

S. Saint Vrain Ave.

Lily
Mtn.
9,712'

ROCKY
MOUNTAIN
NATIONAL PARK

P

Early in the trail the landscape also includes aspen trees and consistent light filtering through them. The trail takes an uncharacteristic dip and then flattens out before ascending a small man-made staircase and starting a series of small switchbacks. As the trail crests, the Estes Park Valley, Marys Lake, and the southern portion of the town of Estes Park come into view. Pass a natural break in the trail that has been carved by hikers going off trail to the right, and continue to the left. This boulder-shaded spot is a nice place to rest. From this junction, start another gradual climb toward Lily Mountain. The summit is not yet in view. Continue on the trail and pass more large rocks and a picturesque dead tree that stands as a sentinel on the right after a large switchback.

At a large outcropping of boulders, you'll see an overlook on the right. Look to the left for views of Rocky Mountain National Park and to the right for more views of the Estes Park Valley and the town of Estes Park. Get back on the trail and continue to climb. The trail becomes dark and shaded, with a forest of large pine trees clustered together.

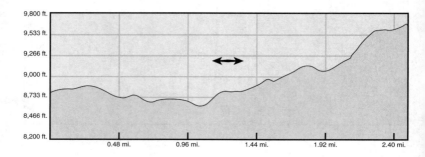

This view is toward the west from the summit of Lily Mountain with a dusting of snow on the Continental Divide.

As the trail continues to ascend with switchbacks, there are built-in erosion-control devices, mainly logs and landscaping materials, along the path. This side of the ridge can be very windy, and you will hear the wind whipping through the dense lodgepole pines. You'll also hear the sounds of the highway far below.

Pass a trail marker at the crest of the hill. Continue to the right toward Lily Mountain's peak, which consists of a large rock pile. Cairns mark the route to the top, and hikers must scramble up this last part of the trail.

Views from the top are extraordinary and include Longs Peak, Twin Sisters, and the Mummy Range. After photographs, have lunch, take a rest, and turn around to retrace the same route.

DIRECTIONS   From Estes Park, go south on CO 7, past Marys Lake. The road curves sharply. After 4.8 miles, look for a small parking area on the right shoulder of the road and a Lily Mountain Trail marker. There is limited roadside parking. Dogs are allowed on this trail.

GPS TRAILHEAD COORDINATES
N40°18.690' W105°32.086'

19 Longs Peak Trailhead: *Longs Peak*

SCENERY: ✿ ✿ ✿ ✿

DIFFICULTY: ✿ ✿ ✿ ✿ ✿

TRAIL CONDITION: ✿ ✿ ✿

DISTANCE: 15 miles out-and-back

CHILDREN: ✿

SOLITUDE: ✿ ✿

HIKING TIME: 12 hours

FLOOD IMPACT: ✿ North Longs Peak Trail is not featured here, but the trail is missing where North Longs Peak Trail and Boulder Book intersect. We note this because the trail name could be misleading and this route originates from Longs Peak Trailhead.

OUTSTANDING FEATURES: Fourteener, evergreen forest, lakes, spectacular mountain views, tundra, waterfalls

AUTHOR'S NOTE: I often hesitate to put this hike in my books before I decide that omitting it would be irresponsible, as Longs Peak is one of Colorado's most popular fourteeners. However, it is also one of the deadliest. The reason? People die on this iconic climb because they are not completely prepared—from novice hikers to the most experienced climbers. Longs Peak claimed its 60th victim in 2014. The 59th person to die on this hike was an experienced mountaineer whose body was recovered by helicopter, three days after he summited, 600 feet below the Ledges section of the Keyhole Route.

Other victims were claimed by lightning, heart attacks, hypothermia, exhaustion, exposure, and even suicide. This number does not include the hundreds that get hurt, lost, or require other service from park rangers or search and rescue every year. I've heard from other hiking experts and park rangers that out of the 15,000 people who attempt to summit each year, only 50% are successful.

My best advice: If you go to Longs Peak, know that you do not have to summit. Stay within your ability and comfort zone. Longs Peak is all about the journey. Turn back in the case of thunder, lightning, rain, snow, hail, high winds, altitude sickness, dehydration, injury, disorientation, summit fever, or overcrowding.

THE EXCURSION UP THIS AWE-INSPIRING mountain blurs the lines between a hike and a climb. The 15 miles will likely rank among the most spectacular yet well-earned miles you have ever hiked. This mountain displays both imposing stature and magnificent beauty that validate its popularity. Longs Peak is the tallest mountain in Rocky Mountain National Park and the fourteener that sits farthest north in Colorado. It is also the easternmost point of the Continental Divide.

Leave the trailhead, follow the East Longs Peak Trail (Keyhole Route), and begin an enchanting jaunt through the trees. Pass a small campground named Goblins Forest. At 1.9 miles, reach a well-constructed bridge crossing over a small, cascading waterfall. This is a beautiful place to take a break.

Your first views of Longs Peak are here as the trees are replaced by shorter vegetation. At 2.5 miles, there is a fork in the trail. Follow the sign left toward the summit. After another mile, you'll reach the junction of the Chasm Lake Trail. This is another great spot to rest, because there is a pit

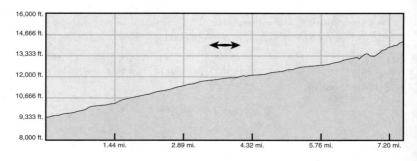

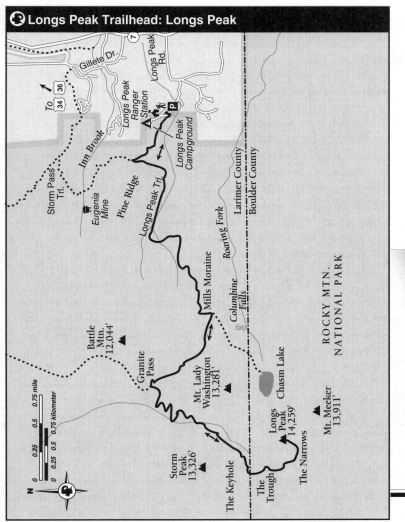

Longs Peak Trailhead: Longs Peak

To 34 36

Gillette Dr.

7

Longs Peak Rd.

Longs Peak Ranger Station

P

Inn Brook

Longs Peak Campground

Storm Pass Trl.

Eugenia Mine

Pine Ridge

Longs Peak Trl

Mills Moraine

Roaring Fork

Larimer County
Boulder County

Columbine Falls

Battle Mtn. 12,044'

Granite Pass

Mt. Lady Washington 13,281'

Chasm Lake

ROCKY MTN. NATIONAL PARK

Mt. Meeker 13,911'

Storm Peak 13,326'

The Keyhole

The Trough

Longs Peak 14,259'

The Narrows

N

0   0.25   0.5   0.75 mile
0   0.25   0.5   0.75 kilometer

toilet and a vista of the east Diamond face of Longs Peak. Head northwest as the trail skirts up Mount Lady Washington to Granite Pass.

Stay left and hike southwest for 1.7 miles to the boulder field, where you'll find another pit toilet and several rock shelters that act as a windbreak for tents. The boulders here are the size of cars. Begin to scramble your way straight up toward the Keyhole. At the base of the boulder field, the top of Longs Peak, the Keyhole, and the expanse of the boulder field are visible.

Many people choose to backpack this far to make for a shorter climb the next day. All campers must obtain a backcountry/wilderness permit. Be warned that you are camping well above treeline and the surface area is 100% rock.

The impressive view of the Longs Peak summit is highlighted here by a rock formation aptly dubbed the Keyhole. At the Keyhole is a small, stone shelter. The terrain becomes significantly more difficult beyond the Keyhole, so take a moment to evaluate the time, the weather, and your physical condition. There is no shame in turning back if conditions are not exactly right, so don't let pride outweigh any safety concerns.

Cross through the Keyhole to the west side of the ridge and take in the expansive view of Glacier Gorge. The trail is now marked by bull's-eyes painted on the rocks. The remainder of the trail is extremely slick when wet and very exposed to the elements. A fall here could be fatal. Follow the exposed ledge for a little more than a quarter mile to a large couloir called the Trough. Ascend the Trough to the top of the west ridge.

Now the trail will traverse east across Longs Peak's south face using a ledge called the Narrows. Like its name suggests, this ledge is narrow—only one hiker wide—and exposed. Take your time and stay calm.

The Homestretch is just beyond the Narrows. It leads you northeast along a series of steep, slick, angled slabs. Be mindful of loose rock; tread lightly, and watch for rock kicked loose by other hikers. In a short while, the summit of Longs Peak seems to magically appear. This airy pinnacle is large and flat. The commanding panorama is well-deserved compensation for your sweat and tired legs. At 14,255 feet, there are plenty of photo opportunities.

After celebrating your lofty accomplishment, turn around and head back the way you came. The ascent will most likely be crowded, which can be a problem on the narrow ledges where hikers cannot pass each other, so be careful.

Note: Hiking time and terrain warrant extra consideration when preparing for this outing. A headlamp is useful for an early start, which is essential for a successful completion of this hike. Many hikers begin as early as 2 a.m. Since this is a long trek, bring ample layers of clothing and extra food and water. As always, tell someone where you're going and when you expect to be back. Crowds of hikers fill this trail every day, so be prepared for a lot of human contact. Snow is often found on this hike, especially through the Trough portion, at any time during the hiking season. I recommend hiking Longs Peak in June through October.

Overnight Option: Longs Peak Campground

Go to bed early. The Park Service recommends that you try to leave the trailhead between 3 a.m. and 6 a.m. to make it to the summit of Longs Peak by noon. Bad weather can occur at any time but is more likely in the afternoon during the summer. Bring plenty of warm clothes and plenty of lung power. The round-trip takes between 12 and 15 hours. Make sure to keep your campsite a second night because you will be too exhausted to do anything except make supper and hit the sack.

This tents-only camping area is located in a scenic setting adjacent to some of the most beautiful mountain land in the Rockies. There are many sights to see and things to do, but the very things that attract you to this park also attract many other visitors. Longs Peak is an extremely popular hike here. Cars will line the road leading to the trailhead and campground. It takes a combination of timing and luck to get a campsite during the peak season, which is from late June through mid-September. All sites are first come, first served. Despite the hustle and bustle nearby, the 26-site campground is still relatively quiet.

The trailhead parking area, however, will have all the action. Pass the line of parked cars along Longs Peak Road and come to a split in the road. Turn right and enter the campground. To your left is the trailhead parking, which tends to be full during summer. The teardrop-shaped gravel

Longs Peak Sunrise Part II, and another reminder that an early start helps hikers navigate the crowds and the weather here.

campground loop makes its way beneath a lodgepole woodland pocked with boulders and smaller trees. The campsites are mostly on the outside of the loop and have somewhat obstructed views of the Twin Sisters peaks across the Tahosa Valley in the Roosevelt National Forest.

More campsites are stretched along the peak side of the loop. As popular as they are, they are well maintained. A hill rises against the campground. This is the campground's rockier side; campsites are more spread out over here. Overall, the sites are average in size, with ample room for the average tent. But always being full does make the place feel a bit confined. Colorful tents and colorful people give Longs Peak some extra pizzazz.

DIRECTIONS From Estes Park, go south on CO 7, past Marys Lake. The road curves sharply and travels to the Longs Peak Trailhead turnoff. Turn right here and travel 1 mile to the Longs Peak Trailhead.

GPS TRAILHEAD COORDINATES
N40°16.195' W105°33.408'

20 Longs Peak Trailhead:
Storm Pass to Estes Cone

SCENERY: ✿ ✿ ✿ ✿

DIFFICULTY: ✿ ✿ ✿ ✿

TRAIL CONDITION: ✿ ✿ ✿ ✿

DISTANCE: 6.7 miles out-and-back

FLOOD IMPACT: **0**

CHILDREN: ✿ ✿

SOLITUDE: ✿ ✿ ✿

HIKING TIME: 3½ hours

OUTSTANDING FEATURES: Shaded evergreen forest with spectacular mountain views at the top

ESTES CONE IS AN INACTIVE VOLCANO CONE. In this book we will profile the trail from Longs Peak Trailhead, even though there are two other access points to Estes Cone. This mostly shaded trail is a nice hike in the summer. It's also a good hike early or late in the season, when some other nearby hikes are thick with snow or even impassable. Estes Cone is a Rocky Mountain National Park hike that can be accessed here without an entrance fee.

🥾🥾 Follow Longs Peak Trail from behind the little ranger's display and miniature museum at the parking lot. Please stop to sign in at the trail register right by the trailhead. Immediately ascend the well-maintained, man-made stairs. Since the trail is in Rocky Mountain National Park, hikers can expect a well-kept path throughout this hike, although the last half mile is rocky, steep, and hard to navigate.

The first half mile of trail is a steady, moderate grade that intersects with Storm Pass Trail. Take a right here onto Storm Pass Trail and follow the signs to Estes Cone.

The trail slowly gives way to loose rock and exposed tree roots. The grade varies as well, including some short descents, and traverses below Pine Ridge. Cross Inn Brook using a log bridge and continue to the right of an

Longs Peak Trailhead: Storm Pass to Estes Cone

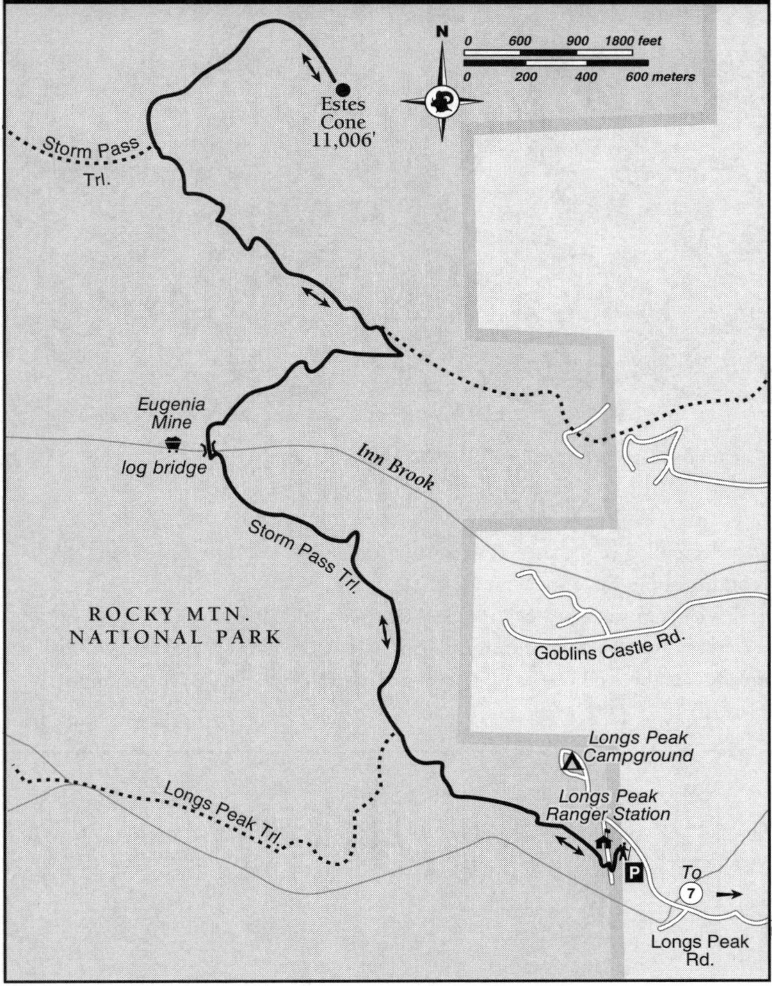
N
0 600 900 1800 feet
0 200 400 600 meters
Estes Cone 11,006'
Storm Pass Trl.
Eugenia Mine
log bridge
Inn Brook
Storm Pass Trl.
ROCKY MTN. NATIONAL PARK
Goblins Castle Rd.
Longs Peak Campground
Longs Peak Ranger Station
Longs Peak Trl.
P
To 7
Longs Peak Rd.

A natural tree artifact from the edges of the Estes Cone Trail

abandoned log cabin site with a rusted boiler and tailings. This is all that remains of the Eugenia Mine.

The trail starts a descent that might seem a little out of place, since our goal is to travel to a summit. Continue to drop down and cross a small meadow as the trail opens up to views of Twin Sisters and our destination,

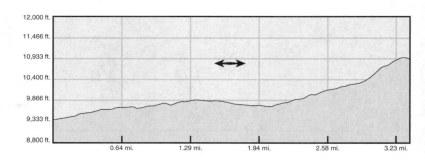

Estes Cone. The trail becomes sandy and smooth. Pass the Moore Park campsites, and at mile 2 you will reach a spur trail. Take a left, follow the signs to Estes Cone, and begin a sharp ascent toward Storm Pass. It is from this point that the trail makes up for lost time and gains most of its elevation.

Spectacular views are to the left—the mountain to your far left is Mount Meeker. Longs Peak can be spotted poking above the ridge, with the peak's diamond facing the trail.

Your lungs will begin to tire as the elevation climbs and the trees become visibly shorter and stunted. At 2.5 miles, you reach the pass, marked by large rock cairns and signs. The Storm Pass Cutoff, to the right, is accessed at the Lily Lake Trailhead. Follow the signs to Estes Cone Trail, bearing right up through rock cairns and the stunted evergreens that dot the hillside. Estes Cone is straight ahead, and once out of the trees, the trail begins to ascend the cone's southwest flank.

The trail is steep and rocky, with twisted and stunted wind-worn trees—take a close look at them and you'll see lightning damage.

Continue to follow the cairns as you pick your way through a vertical rock garden for the last half mile. Eventually, reach a small flat area, then head up and right, scrambling through rocks to the summit of Estes Cone. You are rewarded with magnificent views of Estes Park, Rocky Mountain National Park, Longs Peak, and Mount Meeker. But you should head down, back to the trailhead, before afternoon lightning storms return, as they do most of the summer.

The trailhead has restrooms, campsites, picnic facilities, and a museum, which has plentiful information on hikes and Rocky Mountain National Park. There is also a ranger station that usually has someone on duty.

This hike shares a trailhead with Longs Peak Trail, a very popular hike. Many people start Longs Peak Trail at 4 a.m. or 5 a.m., finishing in early evening. Parking is limited, sometimes freeing up in the afternoon. However, an early start is recommended because lightning storms are common after 12 p.m. The best months to hike here are May through October.

Sometimes the view is obscured by what is in the foreground, as it is with this magnificent natural boulder sculpture at the top of the Estes Cone.

DIRECTIONS   From Estes Park, turn left off US 36 onto CO 7 before the town's first stoplight. Go south on CO 7, past Marys Lake. The road curves sharply and travels to the Longs Peak Trailhead turnoff. Turn right here and travel 1 mile to the Longs Peak Trailhead.

GPS TRAILHEAD COORDINATES

N40°16.195' W105°33.408'

21 Sandbeach Lake Trailhead: *Sandbeach Lake*

SCENERY: ✰ ✰ ✰ ✰

DIFFICULTY: ✰ ✰ ✰

TRAIL CONDITION: ✰ ✰ ✰

DISTANCE: 9 miles out-and-back

CHILDREN: ✰ ✰ ✰

SOLITUDE: ✰ ✰ ✰ ✰

HIKING TIME: 5 hours

FLOOD IMPACT: ✰ ✰ Sandbeach Bridge at Hunters Creek was destroyed, but has since been replaced. Other trail damage is still noticeable but passable.

OUTSTANDING FEATURES: Unique alpine lake setting, headwaters of Sandbeach Creek, views of North St. Vrain Creek drainage, Campers Creek, Hunters Creek

THE SANDY SHORE OF SANDBEACH LAKE is a nice reward for this uphill trek. And that's a good thing, since the elevation gain on this hike is almost 2,000 feet. Its trailhead location, nestled in the south side of Mount Meeker, is a quiet setting for a day hike or an overnight camping trip. The Wild Basin area, near Allenspark, is usually not crowded and is reminiscent of the earlier days in the park. Sandbeach Lake Trail is an easy trail to follow since there are four landmarks that are spaced pretty evenly apart. The first is a trail intersection at 1.5 miles. There's a creek crossing a mile later, a second creek crossing after another mile, and the lake is one final mile away.

🚶🚶 Starting from the parking lot, the trail switches back a few times and continues through the forest along Copeland Moraine. Reach a ridgetop after 1.5 miles, pass an intersection with the Meeker Park trails, and take a left. The trail is very rocky and continues to travel along the ridge in this first section. Copeland Lake is visible on the left.

As you climb and the trail rises steeply from the valley, be sure to look back to the left for views of the North St. Vrain Creek drainage, filled with

Sandbeach Lake Trailhead: Sandbeach Lake

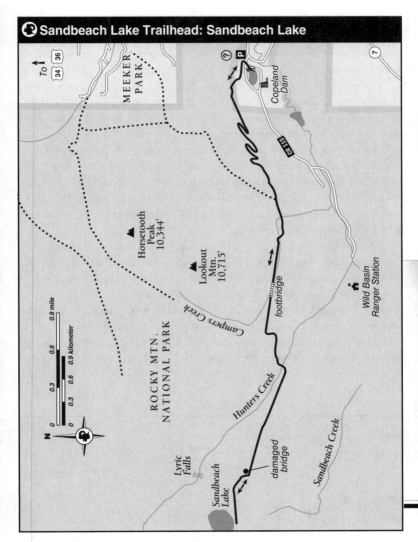

beaver ponds. To the west are views of Mount Copeland. We hiked in the fall when the colors were turning along the trail and in the entire drainage area. The aspen trees were golden, while the brush along the drainage was already a blaze of orange and red.

Pass the Hole in the Wall Campsite. The trail is now flat and very sandy. Continue west along the Sandbeach Lake Trail as it passes alongside Lookout Mountain. Rock outcroppings tower above the trail as it travels along a sandy path that leads through a forest of spruce and pine trees.

Pass Campers Creek Campsite, almost a mile from the Meeker Park intersection. Travel along the shaded creek, down a sharp descent. Cross the waters of Campers Creek on a footbridge and then go back up the hill on the other side of the creek. Pass Beaver Mill Campsite and Hunters Creek Campsite. You will then cross the actual waters of Hunters Creek; you have traveled a mile since the last creek crossing.

West of Hunters Creek, the trail gets steep and climbs another mile to Sandbeach Lake. You'll know you are close when you pass a horse hitch rack on the right. Arrive at Sandbeach Lake. As its namesake suggests, the shoreline is a large, sandy beach. To the north, you can see Longs Peak, Mount Meeker, Keyboard of the Winds, and Pagoda Mountain. There's forest to the west, while the east side is home to the aforementioned sandy shore.

Like many high altitude lakes, Sandbeach Lake was dammed in the early 1900s to help provide water to the Colorado Front Range. The lake was filled

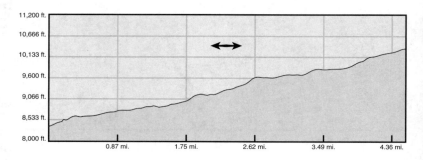

at one point, but the National Park Service bought the reservoir and took apart the dam in the 1980s. The sandy shore was exposed at that time when the water receded.

After a visit to the shore and a nice rest, turn back around the way that you came and return to the trailhead. There is a group campsite and an individual campsite close to Sandbeach Lake. If you'd rather extend your hike and take advantage of the unique setting that Sandbeach Lake offers, then get a backcountry permit and stay awhile. Many also use Sandbeach Lake as a jumping-off point for some of the highest mountain summits in Rocky Mountain National Park.

DIRECTIONS   From the junction of US 36 and CO 7 in Estes Park, turn left on CO 7 and drive 12.5 miles to Wild Basin Road. Turn right and drive to the Rocky Mountain National Park Ranger Station. Sandbeach Lake Trailhead is located immediately to the right of the kiosk. Go through the entrance and turn into the parking lot.

GPS TRAILHEAD COORDINATES
N40°13.069' W105°32.035'

22 Wild Basin Trailhead:
Ouzel Lake Campsite

SCENERY: ✿ ✿ ✿ ✿ ✿ CHILDREN: ✿

DIFFICULTY: ✿ ✿ ✿ ✿ SOLITUDE: ✿ ✿ ✿ ✿ ✿

TRAIL CONDITION: ✿ ✿ ✿ ✿ HIKING TIME: 5 hours

DISTANCE: 9.8 miles out-and-back

FLOOD IMPACT: ✿ ✿ ✿ Ouzel Falls bridge was destroyed and has not been replaced. The spur trail to Ouzel Lake is damaged, and the bridge is also gone. A detour to Ouzel, Bluebird, and Thunder Lakes is posted on the trail.

OUTSTANDING FEATURES: Waterfalls and water cascades: Copeland Falls, Calypso Cascades, and Ouzel Falls; privacy; alpine lake

THE OUZEL LAKE CAMPSITE lies in a spruce-fir forest below the northeastern slope of Copeland Mountain. You'd be hard-pressed to find many people here or on the trail, save for a few anglers above Calypso Cascades and a smattering of hikers. Constantly thundering waterfalls and cascades along the creeks, especially during spring runoff, are impressive sights and sounds you'll encounter along the entire route.

🏃 From the parking lot the trail immediately crosses a bridge over Hunters Creek. The trail is wide, fairly smooth, dirt, and level. Travel through lodgepole-pine trees and aspen trees. Less than a half mile from the trailhead is Copeland Falls, a sudden drop in North St. Vrain Creek. A social trail to the left of the main trail leads hikers to Copeland Falls. Take the detour to see both the upper and lower falls, and then rejoin the main trail.

After passing Copeland Falls, the trail narrows. Pass an intersection with a backcountry campsite trail and continue straight, following the signs to Calypso Cascades and Ouzel Falls. Cross North St. Vrain Creek on a sturdy

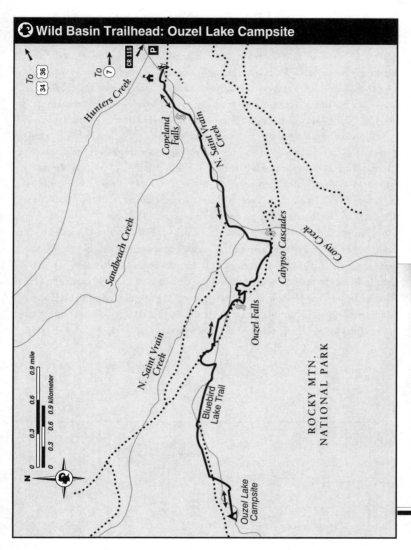

Wild Basin Trailhead: Ouzel Lake Campsite

To 34 36

To 7

CR 115

P

Hunters Creek

Copeland Falls

N. Saint Vrain Creek

Sandbeach Creek

Calypso Cascades

Cony Creek

Ouzel Falls

N. Saint Vrain Creek

Bluebird Lake Trail

Ouzel Lake Campsite

ROCKY MTN. NATIONAL PARK

0.9 mile
0.6
0.3
0.9 kilometer
0.6
0.3
0

N

wood-and-stone bridge, complete with deafening falls in the springtime. Follow the trail uphill as it continues through the forest along Cony Creek to Calypso Cascades. This water feature is named for the namesake orchid that blooms here in July. Trails intersect at Calypso Cascades, and hikers turn right, cross twin bridges, go around a bend, and then cross a third bridge.

You'll still see damage here from the Ouzel Fire, a well-known forest fire in 1978, but by now shrubs and flowers are plentiful in spot-burn areas.

Your hike will become quieter as you leave the water behind. Climb a series of wide switchbacks as you take in views of the surrounding mountain peaks. From right to left, the first peak is the south side of Mount Meeker, with a good view of its sharp ridge along the top. Next to that is the south side of Longs Peak. To your left, you will see a tremendous amount of downed timber and small landslides up on the hillside.

The distant sounds of the falls are a constant reminder of the water in this area, but be patient—there's an uphill climb and more switchbacks before the next water views. Ouzel Falls is next, and it ranks as one of the most popular falls in Rocky Mountain National Park. Cross the trail's bridge spanning Ouzel Creek. Stop in the middle of the bridge to see the upper part of the falls, which is a sheer drop. In a minute or two, you'll come across a rock outcropping that makes for a great resting place, with expansive views to the east.

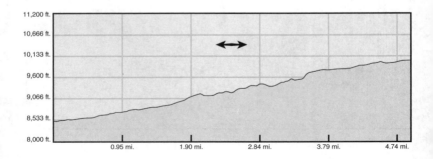

After crossing Ouzel Creek, the trail circles below the ridge where Ouzel Falls drops. Switchbacks wind downhill through boulders and under an overhanging cliff. At the next trail junction, take a left and continue to Ouzel Lake. This is Bluebird Lake Trail; it climbs to a crest and then becomes relatively straight and level, but also narrower and rocky. This next section is extremely exposed—definitely not where you want to be during a storm. The views to the right are Tanima Peak and Mount Alice.

At the next trail intersection, take a left onto the spur trail to the Ouzel Lake Campsite. Wind downhill and rejoin Ouzel Creek. Travel along the creek until you see the outhouse for the Ouzel Lake Campsite. The campsite is just before Ouzel Lake, so if you've reached the lake, you've gone too far. Climb the stairs, pass the outhouse, proceed 150 feet, and you will be at the official tent site. A small trail continues west of the campsite, joins with the main trail, and leads to Ouzel Lake and a bear-proof container where campers can store their food for the night.

Ouzel Lake itself is dominated by Copeland Mountain. The other beauties visible from the lake are the Ouzel and Manaha peaks. After a restful night, get up and go back the way that you came.

DIRECTIONS   From Estes Park and the junction of US 36 and CO 7, drive south on CO 7 via Marys Lake Road 12.5 miles to Wild Basin Road. Turn right, drive past the Wild Basin Inn, and take the right-hand fork to the Entrance Station. Travel another 3 miles to the Ranger Station and Wild Basin Trailhead.

GPS TRAILHEAD COORDINATES
N40°12.336' W105°33.862'

WEST SIDE OF
ROCKY MOUNTAIN
NATIONAL PARK

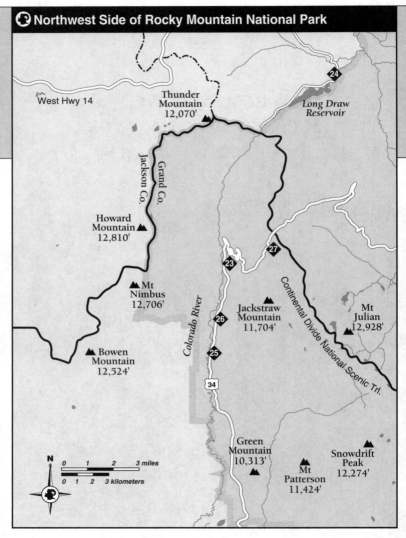

Northwest Side of Rocky Mountain National Park

West Hwy 14

Thunder Mountain
12,070'

Long Draw Reservoir

24

Jackson Co.

Grand Co.

Howard Mountain ▲▲
12,810'

Mt Nimbus ▲▲
12,706'

23

27

Continental Divide National Scenic Trl.

Mt Julian ▲
12,928'

26

Colorado River

Jackstraw Mountain
11,704'

Bowen Mountain ▲
12,524'

25

34

N

0   1   2   3 miles
0   1   2   3 kilometers

Green Mountain
10,313'

Mt Patterson
11,424'

Snowdrift Peak ▲
12,274'

OVERLEAF: HIKE 30 *Tonahutu Creek Trail to Renegade Campsite to Flattop Mountain (see page 168). Cairns dot the landscape of many of the west side hikes in Rocky Mountain National Park, as seen here on the trek to Renegade Campsite.*

NORTHWEST SIDE OF ROCKY MOUNTAIN NATIONAL PARK
(Trail Ridge Road, Colorado River Headwaters Area, and Never Summer Range)

HIKE 27 *Continental Divide Trail to Mount Ida (see page 152). Wildlife is plentiful on the west side of the park. Here, a herd of bighorn sheep graze on the Continental Divide*

Note on Flood Impact: The west side of Rocky Mountain National Park was largely unaffected by the storm, with the flood occurring only east of the Continental Divide. Therefore, the hikes on the west side are not rated for flood impact.

23 Colorado River Trailhead:
Colorado River Trail to Lulu City

SCENERY: ✿ ✿ ✿ ✿

DIFFICULTY: ✿ ✿

TRAIL CONDITION: ✿ ✿ ✿ ✿

DISTANCE: 7.4 miles out-and-back

CHILDREN: ✿ ✿ ✿

SOLITUDE: ✿ ✿ ✿ ✿

HIKING TIME: 3½ hours

OUTSTANDING FEATURES: Mining history, Colorado River,
Never Summer Mountains, meadows

LULU CITY IS AN OLD MINING TOWN that no longer exists, but the ghosts still linger. This trail maps the route to the town, passing old cabins and the mountain views the 200 or so residents would have seen in the late 1800s. The trail is level and follows the Colorado River, with constant views of the mountain ridges of the Never Summers.

🥾 Leave the trailhead from the north side of the parking lot. Large evergreen trees shade the wide dirt trail. Cross over a footbridge and officially enter Rocky Mountain National Park. Head up a set of switchbacks that will get your blood moving. This little climb is deceiving because the majority of the trail is level or gradually ascending, with only a total 200-foot elevation change to the turnaround point. There are man-made steps along the trail, and just as quickly as you go up, you come down again.

The Colorado River is to your left. Cross two bridges; the first is a split-log bridge and the second is a wider bridge. Reach the banks of the river, and the trail begins to travel along the river for a short time. There are many social trails that cut through to access the water.

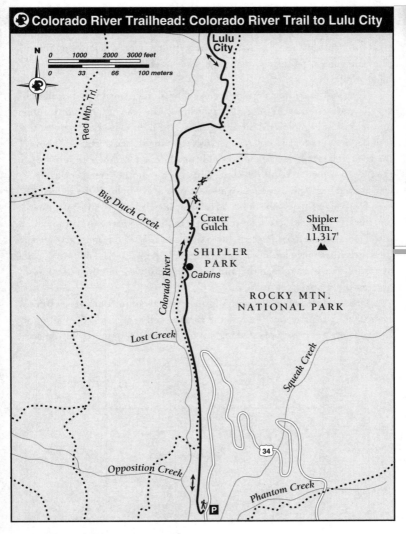

☸ Colorado River Trailhead: Colorado River Trail to Lulu City

Lulu City

Red Mtn. Trl.

Big Dutch Creek

Crater Gulch

SHIPLER PARK
Cabins

Colorado River

Shipler Mtn. 11,317'

ROCKY MTN. NATIONAL PARK

Lost Creek

Squeak Creek

34

Opposition Creek

Phantom Creek

N

0   1000   2000   3000 feet
0   33   66   100 meters

135

The Colorado River conjures up visions of thundering rapids and towering canyons for most, but right here is the birthplace of the river. It's a great opportunity to see the waterway in a unique light, as a gurgling infant, calm and gentle, gathering up enough water to ebb and flow through the high country.

The landscape opens up for a short time along a small meadow. Reach a trail intersection at the edge of the meadow. Go straight here, continuing up the trail heading toward Shipler Cabins and Lulu City. At this point the trail begins a gradual ascent and narrows to a singletrack, traversing above the river. The trail passes below an old rockslide; a meadow with new views of the surrounding peaks is to the left. Cross below another small rockslide; the trail is level here and easy to navigate as it proceeds north up the valley.

Pass a sign for Crater Creek, cross over it via a bridge, and continue. Shortly after Crater Creek, on the right, are the remains of the Shipler Cabins. These two tumbled log structures sit at the edge of Shipler Park—imagine the killer views they had, not to mention the killer winters! The trail continues to follow the stage road that ran through Lulu City and then northwest over mountain passes to Walden.

Cross a series of bridges and begin a gradual climb. Dense trees once again shade the path, but you lose the views as well as access to the Colorado River. There are now roots sticking out of the dirt path, but it's still in great

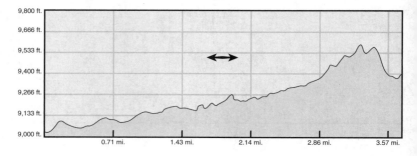

*The Colorado River's birthplace is on this trail, and the many small trickles of water,
pictured here, can be seen on the trail to Lulu City.*

condition and easy to follow. As the trail ascends, a drop-off on the left side begins to develop, the forest gets very dense, and it becomes eerily quiet.

At the intersection of Little Yellowstone Canyon, Little Ditch, and La Poudre Pass, take a left on the trail headed downhill to Lulu City. The trail continues to descend with switchbacks and a stream crossing, and then levels out again. A sign marks the Lulu City Site (1879–1884, population 200). Don't go looking for a ghost town, remarkable mining, or log-cabin relics. The only memories here are written in the winds. From here, turn around and go back the way that you came.

DIRECTIONS From the Grand Lake Entrance Station, take US 34 east 9.6 miles. Turn left into the Colorado River Trailhead parking lot.

GPS TRAILHEAD COORDINATES
N40°24.000' W105°50.879'

24 Corral Creek Trailhead:
Poudre River Trail to Cache Campsite

SCENERY: ✿✿✿✿✿   CHILDREN: ✿✿

DIFFICULTY: ✿✿✿   SOLITUDE: ✿✿✿✿✿

TRAIL CONDITION: ✿   HIKING TIME: 6 hours

DISTANCE: 11.7 miles out-and-back

OUTSTANDING FEATURES: Rivers, creeks, wildlife, high mountain peaks, unique access on north side of Rocky Mountain National Park

---

A BETTER CAMPSITE COULDN'T BE DREAMT UP. Cache Campsite is close to perfect. It is tucked into the trees at the edge of a mountain meadow in a high valley, surrounded by mountain peaks with a river running through it. This moderate 5.85-mile hike to Cache along the Cache la Poudre River is also a gem in its own right. There are open valleys and plentiful big game, especially deer and moose.

🚶🚶 From the trailhead, proceed straight across the bridge. A sign indicates it's 1 mile to the Rocky Mountain National Park boundary. The trail is an old doubletrack jeep road in spots, and a singletrack in others. Pass the boundary marker for Comanche Peak Wilderness. Head into a slight descent and follow the creek downstream. Pass wetlands, coniferous forests, and the intermittent views of the surrounding peaks. The trail is easy to follow.

Move quickly through the wetlands to avoid mosquitoes. Continue to follow La Poudre Pass Creek, which flows out of Long Draw Reservoir, downstream about a mile to its confluence with the Cache la Poudre River. The trail surface is soft dirt with occasional roots or rocks.

Bear right at the intersection with the Big South Trail. The Big South Trail heads north to CO 14 and has its own trailhead there.

Cross the bridge over the Cache la Poudre River, obviously bigger than La Poudre Pass Creek. Continue straight at the intersection with Mummy Pass Trail, following the signs to Chapin Creek. Hague Campsite is immediately to the left, which I don't recommend since it's infested with mosquitoes.

This first half mile is extremely easy and follows the gentle grade of the river. Pay attention as the trail all but disappears in the wetland flats along the riverbank. Stay close to the river. When in doubt, remember that the trail eventually climbs up an embankment and away from the river. Hikers eventually come back near the river, looking down upon it as it cascades through a mini-gorge. Catch your breath and follow the trail uphill for a short steep ascent. Hike another mile and continue on the trail as you emerge into a pristine valley. The trail is little worn through this valley, but easier to follow because the trees are not as dense. Pass any spur trails or social trails and follow the trail up the valley. The trail climbs a small bluff, and the top is a great place to stop for views and a rest. Continue straight after descending from the little bluff.

The trail disappears but continues straight across the marshy area; continue to pay attention as the trail will veer right. Climb into the woods, where carpet-like undergrowth covers the forest, and your views temporarily vanish. The trail is very obvious here; follow it south. After a short descent, the trail is back down closer to river level. Travel a few hundred yards as the river bends off to the left and hikers continue straight, away from the river. The

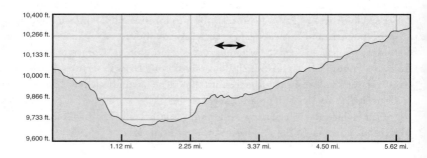

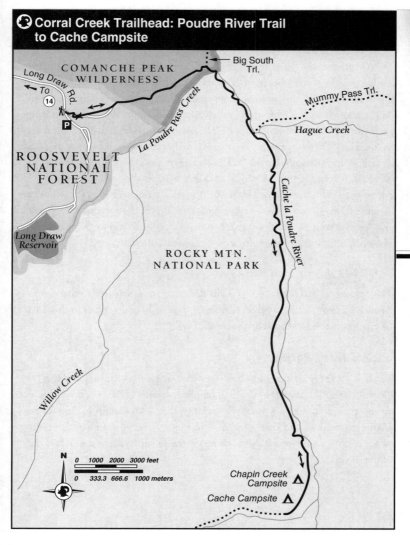

Corral Creek Trailhead: Poudre River Trail to Cache Campsite

COMANCHE PEAK WILDERNESS

Big South Trl.

Long Draw Rd.

→ To (14)

P

La Poudre Pass Creek

Mummy Pass Trl.

Hague Creek

ROOSVEVELT NATIONAL FOREST

Cache la Poudre River

Long Draw Reservoir

ROCKY MTN. NATIONAL PARK

Willow Creek

N

0   1000 2000 3000 feet
0   333.3 666.6 1000 meters

Chapin Creek Campsite △

Cache Campsite △

trail begins to ascend. (It should be easy to see that you're on the right path here.) Exit the trees and enjoy the views of another large valley surrounded by mountain peaks.

Continue straight at an old sign indicating Chapin Creek Campsite to the left. Cache is straight ahead. The trail travels in and out of the trees, along the western edge of the meadow. The creek you can see now is Chapin Creek. As you walk along the edge of the valley, keep an eye out for the Cache Campground sign—it's easy to miss. Signs indicate two separate tent sites. Both are in the trees. The campsite on the right is fairly spacious compared to most of the Rocky Mountain National Park backcountry sites. We camped here, and although it is in the trees, it is only 100 feet from the edge of the meadow. The campsite to the left is a little farther off the trail, not quite as large, but deeper into the trees. Campers may wish to sit at the edge of the meadow as it gets dark and see who your neighbors are. When we camped, two moose came to call. Have fun camping and leave the way you came in the morning.

TAKE NOTE: *Alternate Access*

The Poudre Lake Trailhead, off Trail Ridge Road, is an alternate to the Poudre Canyon access. It gives hikers a 5.6-mile hike downhill to the Cache Campsite in Rocky Mountain National Park.

Backcountry Permit

There is an information station where you can get backcountry permits at Corral Creek Trailhead, but it isn't regularly staffed. Hikers will need to plan ahead, pick up their backcountry permit in Rocky Mountain National Park at an earlier time, and then head over to Poudre Canyon. (The backcountry office had no problem with us picking up the permit during a separate trip to the park.)

Trail Condition

The first 1.5 miles of this trail are easy to follow, but then it travels through a series of open valleys and becomes harder to navigate. Some very wet areas and game trails could cause confusion. The trail does go up and away from the river a few times but never for long, so pay attention. When in doubt, keep traveling along the river—eventually you will end up in the final and largest valley. That last section is where the hike skirts the trees, and you'll find Cache Campsite. You shouldn't get too lost here!

DIRECTIONS   From Fort Collins drive north on US 287 for 11 miles to CO 14. Turn left on CO 14 and drive 54 miles west to Long Draw Road. Turn left and travel 8.5 miles on Long Draw Road to the Corral Creek Trailhead on the left. There is an information cabin on the other side of the road.

GPS TRAILHEAD COORDINATES

N40°30.967' W105°46.214'

25 Coyote Valley Trail

SCENERY: ✿ ✿ ✿

DIFFICULTY: ✿

TRAIL CONDITION: ✿ ✿ ✿ ✿

DISTANCE: 1 mile out-and-back

CHILDREN: ✿ ✿ ✿ ✿ ✿

SOLITUDE: ✿ ✿

HIKING TIME: 45 minutes

OUTSTANDING FEATURES: Colorado River, Never Summer Mountains, wildlife, meadow

THIS IS AN EASY TRAIL that offers many rewards. Strollers and wheelchairs glide along without much effort through open meadow along the calm beginnings of the Colorado River. People of all hiking abilities can appreciate the views of the Never Summers, the informative signs, and promise of moose spotting. A great novice trail to get the youngsters interested in hiking, it's also a good one to keep the young-at-heart out on the trail.

🚶🚶 Leave the parking area and travel to the trailhead kiosk. There are also restroom facilities here, adjacent to the parking area. The trail is packed dirt, mostly level, and is wheelchair accessible. Pass along a man-made fence and continue over a bridge that spans the Colorado River. The evergreen trees are dense and cooling at the trailhead, but once you cross the bridge the shade is gone as meadowlands appear.

Take a right turn on the interpretive Coyote Valley Trail. To the left is a picnic area with a nicely spaced cluster of picnic tables in the trees. This area is for day use only, and camping and fires are prohibited. Pass one of the many trail benches on the left. The trail continues to follow along the Colorado River. It's still completely level and flanked by thin stands of trees on the right. The meadows of the Kawuneeche Valley are to the left. When we hiked in the summer, the meadow was full of grass and browned by the sun, with patches of wildflowers peeking out.

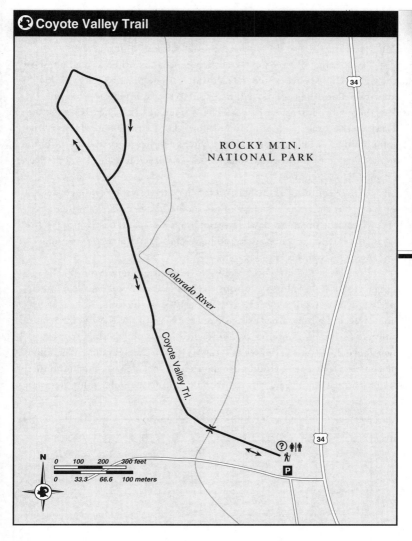

Coyote Valley Trail

ROCKY MTN.
NATIONAL PARK

Colorado River

Coyote Valley Trl.

N

| 0 | 100 | 200 | 300 feet |
| 0 | 33.3 | 66.6 | 100 meters |

34

34

The first interpretive sign hikers approach tells us about the riparian habitat. A colored line drawing shows representations of the water shrew, the American dipper, and the chorus frog—all residents of this area.

Pass a string of three man-made log benches and then a small pond on the right. These benches line the route and offer a place to rest at almost any point along the trail. Social trails lead to the Colorado River shore. Pass three more interpretive signs: The Women of Life, The Visitors to the Kawuneeche, and The Mountain Meadows. Look straight ahead toward the mountains and you'll spot the Grand Ditch. This large, road-like cut in the mountainside is a horizontal canal that diverts precious water from the Never Summers to other areas.

At the beginning of the balloon for the Coyote Valley Trail, go straight, traveling left along the west edge of the trail. This area offers a little more shade from the open meadow. The trail loops along and travels close to the river. It's easy to spot moose around here—the animals like to take long, afternoon rests in these cool marshy areas.

The Never Summers are in full view as the trail loops around. The larger peak is Baker Mountain, with an elevation of 12,397 feet. An interpretive sign speaks of a glacier valley that existed in this area. A sheet of ice, almost 20 miles long, once existed from the head of the Kawuneeche Valley, south to Shadow Mountain Lake. Only the highest peaks visible rose 1,500 feet above the thick layer of ice as it carved this U-shaped valley. When the glacier receded, it left behind huge mounds of rock debris called moraines. Forests now grow in these ridges of rubble around the valley sides. Remnants

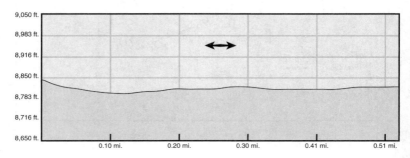

The author and her children on the Coyote Valley Trail

of glacial ice still occupy the east-facing peaks high in the Never Summers to the left, or right, depending where you are in the loop.

The balloon is short and sweet, so get back on the trail and return by the same route. Stop at the picnic area on the way out, or skip rocks in the river.

DIRECTIONS   From the Grand Lake Entrance Station, take US 34 east 5.6 miles to the Coyote Valley Trailhead. Turn left onto the access road and dead-end at the parking lot.

GPS TRAILHEAD COORDINATES
N40°20.557' W105°51.480'

26 Holzwarth Historic Site:
Never Summer Ranch

SCENERY: ✩ ✩ ✩

DIFFICULTY: ✩

TRAIL CONDITION: ✩ ✩ ✩ ✩

DISTANCE: 1.14 miles out-and-back

CHILDREN: ✩ ✩ ✩ ✩ ✩

SOLITUDE: ✩ ✩

HIKING TIME: 45 minutes

OUTSTANDING FEATURES: Colorado River, Never Summer Mountains, meadow, historic buildings, nature walk

THE COLORFUL HISTORY of this amazing little ranch is enough for any hiker to long for the old days. Whether it's the rustic tourist complex created in 1920 (Holzwarth Trout Lodge) or the guest and dude ranch that operated into the 1970s (Never Summer Ranch), you'll wish you would have stayed here. The trail is level and mostly accessible by strollers or wheelchairs. The buildings, however, are not handicapped accessible.

🚶🚶 Begin from the parking area, which accesses the flat, glacially carved Kawuneeche Valley at the foot of the Never Summer Mountains. The rustic buildings that still exist are the final destination on this hike and offer a glimpse into the history of the pioneers of the turn of the 20th century. One of the cabins is located right at the trailhead and was built by a neighboring homesteader and miner. The cabin is equipped on most summer weekend days with a knowledgeable volunteer. All buildings on this hike are open daily from 10 a.m. to 4 p.m., and there are restrooms at the trailhead.

Leave the trailhead cabin and follow the dirt road toward the river and the trees. The trail is a level dirt road. Continue across the valley, looking left and down the Kawuneeche Valley. Interpretive signs throughout the path tell hikers of the Never Summer Ranch.

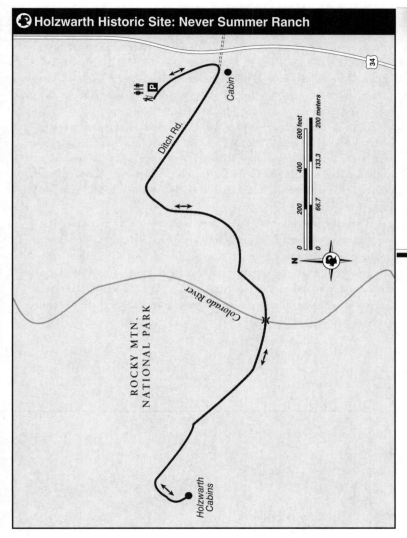

Holzwarth Historic Site: Never Summer Ranch

Ditch Rd.

Cabin

34

Colorado River

ROCKY MTN. NATIONAL PARK

Holzwarth Cabins

N

0   200   400   600 feet

0   66.7   133.3   200 meters

One of the Kawuneeche Valley's first dude ranches once thrived here. In 1917 German immigrants Sophia and John Holzwarth built their homestead here after wartime prohibition closed their saloon in Denver. Originally, ranchers began hosting friends from the city at the Holzwarth Trout Lodge. More visitors followed. The Never Summer Ranch, as it was later known, offered fishing, hunting, and horseback rides. Guests stayed in rustic cabins or a lodge that once stood in the meadow before us.

In 1975, Never Summer Ranch and Holzwarth Homestead became part of Rocky Mountain National Park. Although the newer buildings were removed to restore the meadow, this dirt road leads to the Holzwarths' original homestead buildings. In its historic heyday, the Never Summer Ranch offered horseback riding, hunting, and all the trout you could catch for $2 a day or $11 a week.

The infantile Colorado River flows to the right, where at a mere 10 miles upstream it begins, in a trickle to the Pacific watershed. Pass interpretive signs about moose, which are plentiful in this area. Cross the Colorado River via a bridge. Pass old farm equipment and fence posts, which look like the outline of an old corral. Continue on the road and head into an area that is a little shadier thanks to the evergreen trees that mark the beginning of the ranch.

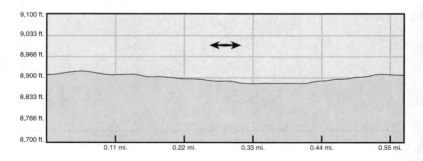

The first signs appear: Holzwarth Trout Lodge, 1920–29, and before you know it, you've made it to the destination. Take time to circle around and tour the buildings. There's a taxidermy shop, kitchens, a bunk house, an ice house, a wood shed, old sleds, wagons, and more. Maybe you can even envision what it would have been like to smell the bacon that Sophia may have been frying up on a cool summer morning. Then close your eyes and dream of the rugged simplicity that characterized the West when it was young. After a look at the historic site, turn around and head back the way you came.

DIRECTIONS   From the Grand Lake Entrance Station, take US 34 east 7.2 miles to the sign for Holzwarth Historic Site. Turn left into the parking lot.

GPS TRAILHEAD COORDINATES
N40°22.247' W105°51.253'

27 Milner Pass Trailhead:
Continental Divide Trail to Mount Ida

SCENERY: ✿ ✿ ✿ ✿   CHILDREN: ✿ ✿

DIFFICULTY: ✿ ✿ ✿ ✿   SOLITUDE: ✿ ✿ ✿ ✿

TRAIL CONDITION: ✿ ✿ ✿   HIKING TIME: 6 hours

DISTANCE: 10 miles out-and-back

OUTSTANDING FEATURES: Alpine tundra, bighorn sheep, elk, summer
tundra wildflowers, expansive views, Continental Divide

A TUNDRA TREK that travels along the crest of the Continental Divide
will bring you to the summit of Mount Ida. Solitude is practically guaranteed
here, along with incredible scenery and the chance to see plenty of wildlife.
Once at the summit, there are also views of the alpine basin of the Gorge
Lakes. Most of the hike is above treeline in open tundra, so leave early and be
willing to turn back if you spot developing storms.

🏃 Milner Pass Trailhead is a busy place, so exit quickly and head toward
Poudre Lake, a small beaver pond to the left of the parking area.

Travel along the Old Fall River Road and the Ute Trail, also an official
Continental Divide landmark. Begin to ascend, switchback, and travel up the
stairs. Pass rock spires on the left as the trail continues to switchback, and travel
along a ridge. You'll still be able to hear the traffic from Trail Ridge Road, but
because the trail ascends quickly, you'll be away from the crowds soon.

The trail levels out for a short while, but you'll still be huffing and
puffing. Cross a split-log bridge over a dry gully and then continue onward
and upward. At the trail junction, approximately a mile from the trailhead,
continue straight, following the sign that says Mount Ida, on the Continental

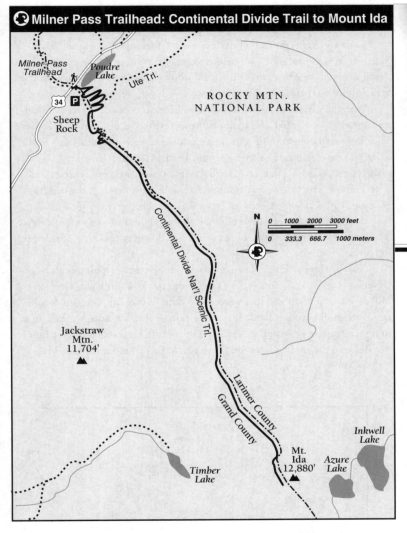

Milner Pass Trailhead: Continental Divide Trail to Mount Ida

Milner Pass Trailhead

Poudre Lake

Ute Trl.

34

P

Sheep Rock

ROCKY MTN. NATIONAL PARK

N

0   1000   2000   3000 feet

0   333.3   666.7   1000 meters

Continental Divide Nat'l Scenic Trl.

Jackstraw Mtn. 11,704'

Larimer County

Grand County

Timber Lake

Mt. Ida 12,880'

Azure Lake

Inkwell Lake

Divide Trail. The large switchback, which goes up the left, takes other hikers toward the Alpine Visitor Center and the Old Fall River Road.

Look to your right in the southwest direction for views of the Never Summer Mountains. The trail begins a descent, making this section of trail much easier. It remains easy as the trail follows a level path through a marshy area and then crosses a split-log bridge.

With the marshy conditions there may be spots of mud. When we hiked in midsummer, we spotted a lot of animal tracks crisscrossing the muddy sections. Rock steps signal the start of your next climbing segment—so much for restful hiking on easy terrain. The trees become dense as this trail continues a milder grade uphill. It is here that we spotted a giant elk with a 12-point antler rack.

Traverse around the hill and begin to walk right through the tundra, cresting at 11,379 feet. After we traversed along the western ridge on our hike, we came upon a group of bighorn sheep—four lambs and eight adults. This appears to be a spot where the sheep bed down, since the tundra grass looks matted down.

Now begins the long, hard trek above timberline, complete with large traverses, switchbacks, and a lot of false summits. You think you've reached Mount Ida, and then you look across and there it is again. Continue on, and if the trail becomes faint, follow the cairns, always heading uphill, in a southern trajectory. You'll be required in spots to scramble over easy boulder fields in the midst of the tundra to reach the summit of Mount Ida at

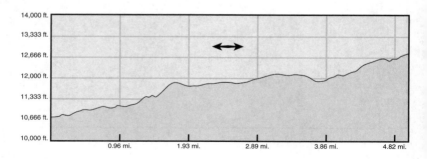

Bighorn sheep are iconic in Rocky Mountain National Park, as are the moose and elk. This herd was spotted on the Continental Divide Trail on the route to Mount Ida.

12,880 feet. From here you see views of Chief Cheley Peak, Cracktop, Mount Julian, and Terra Tomah Mountain. The shimmering waters below form the Gorge Lakes drainage. From here, at a 2,000-foot elevation gain from 10,745 feet, turn around and head back the way that you came.

DIRECTIONS   From the Grand Lake Entrance Station, take US 34 east 16 miles to the Milner Pass Trailhead. Turn right into the parking lot.

GPS TRAILHEAD COORDINATES
N40°25.107' W105°48.651'

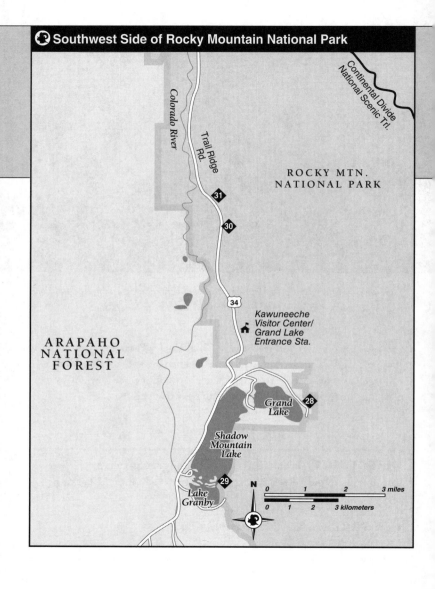

⊙ Southwest Side of Rocky Mountain National Park

Continental Divide National Scenic Trl.

Colorado River

Trail Ridge Rd.

ROCKY MTN. NATIONAL PARK

🔷 31

🔷 30

34

Kawuneeche Visitor Center/ Grand Lake Entrance Sta.

ARAPAHO NATIONAL FOREST

Grand Lake

🔷 28

Shadow Mountain Lake

🔷 29

Lake Granby

N

0   1   2   3 miles

0   1   2   3 kilometers

SOUTHWEST SIDE OF ROCKY MOUNTAIN NATIONAL PARK
(Tonahutu Area, East Inlet Area, and North Inlet Area)

HIKE 30 *Tonahutu Creek Trail to Renegade Campsite to Flattop Mountain (see page 168). A group of backpackers make the journey across Rocky Mountain National Park.*

28 East Inlet Trailhead:
Lake Verna Campsite

SCENERY: ✿ ✿ ✿ ✿ ✿

DIFFICULTY: ✿ ✿ ✿ ✿

TRAIL CONDITION: ✿ ✿ ✿

DISTANCE: 13.8 miles out-and-back

CHILDREN: ✿

SOLITUDE: ✿ ✿ ✿ ✿ ✿

HIKING TIME: 8 hours

OUTSTANDING FEATURES: Creeks, lakes, waterfalls, optimum chance of seeing moose, views of numerous mountain peaks including Mt. Alice and Mt. Craig

AFTER THE FIRST FEW EASY MILES, all with a high probability of seeing moose, the trail becomes steep and takes hikers to a wonderful wooded campsite on a spectacular subalpine lake: Lake Verna. This overnight destination is unique because it's ringed by high alpine peaks, and the campsite itself is the highest elevation of all the campsites on this trial. Lake Verna also signifies the end of the maintained trail; the trail does continue, but it's not maintained by Rocky Mountain National Park.

🚶🚶 The East Portal Trailhead shares a parking lot with the public boat launch, which can be confusing. Leave the trailhead and enter the trail by crossing through a small sagebrush meadow. Cross over a bridge that protects hikers from a low, marshy area and enter a lodgepole-pine forest. Many of the trees here are brownish red because they have been killed by pine beetles.

Pass the spur trail to Adams Falls. Proceed up the rock stairs, half of which are natural and half man-made. The trail is singletrack and hard-packed dirt. You'll pass another entrance to Adams Falls and the Adams Falls Loop, and a minute or two later begin to travel along a small creek.

Don't be discouraged by the damage to the lodgepole pines. On this particular trail, nature has begun to take its restorative course and aspen trees are already filling in the areas vacated by the lodgepole pines.

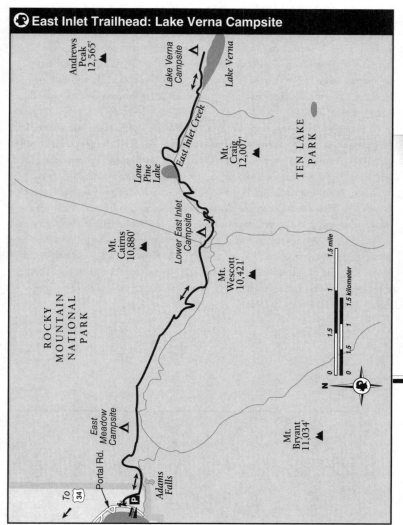

TONAHUTU AREA, EAST INLET AREA, AND NORTH INLET AREA

There are always many day hikers on the first few miles of this trail, and it isn't rare to pass groups with no daypacks or even water supplies. If these hikers ask how far it is to Lake Verna, be sure to warn them that it's almost 7 miles—they might be disillusioned by the ease of the first part of the trail. When we hiked, we even passed a hiker with a walker. (Oddly enough, we noticed the next day that the walker had been abandoned a few miles from the trailhead.)

Pass alongside wetlands, an open meadow full of grasses, and views of the mountain peaks ahead. Continue to follow the trail along the north side of this meadow. The trail will pass through the wetlands for some time. This gives hikers ample opportunity to see the moose that frequent this area.

The trail begins to climb slowly above those meadows. Pass the turnoffs for the East Meadow Campsite. A sign here encourages hikers to stay on the main trail and go 100 yards beyond the turnoff for what the Park Service calls a "prime moose-viewing overlook with wetlands, meadow views, and everything right in front of you." Sure enough, there was a moose walking on the far end of the meadow when we hiked here. They're dark brown and about the size of a large horse, with long legs and a unique walk, and of course those trademark plate antlers.

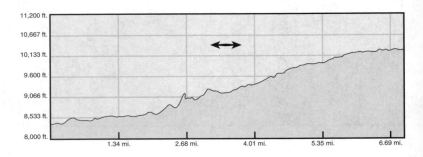

The aptly named Lone Pine Lake on the way to Lake Verna Campsite—aptly named because this hike is solitude defined.

Follow the trail as it climbs into the woods across a tiny, rustic, split-log bridge. The diversity of the trees here—spruce, fir, and pine all reaching toward the sky—makes this trail feel very alive.

You'll come across a longer split-log bridge in 100 yards. When crossing, look for a small waterfall coming off the rocks to the left. A few minutes of climbing will bring you to your next bridge, a little more formal and constructed in style. There is also a great view here of the rock formations above.

From this point forward, the hike gets more difficult and you won't be viewing any more wildlife. As the trail gets steeper past the Lower East Inlet Campsite, look for a nice rock on your right—the perfect spot to rest. Just past this point is a very rocky, steep section of the trail; you'll see another large rock on your left and a drop-off on your right. With your pack on, you'll definitely feel the burn along this path.

Follow the steep and narrow singletrack trail as it continues up along the left-hand wall of this valley.

The valley has slowly narrowed into a gorge. The trail begins to switchback, traveling to the north and then northwest. Wind through the boulders and up the steep man-made rock stairs. A set of downhill stairs follows, as hikers head back toward the creek. Take in the view and the falls. There is a great place to take off your boots and cool your feet in the creek, just beyond the falls.

The next mile is uneventful. Then you might start to notice that, at the base of some of the trees in this area, the bark has been stripped away. When I hiked here, I noticed a squirrel high in a tree, ripping off pieces of bark, which fell down on me like rain.

Cross another split-log bridge and look to the left, where another beautiful waterfall is tumbling down the face of a rock. Continue on and eventually views of higher peaks come into frame. Cross a wood-and-stone bridge over East Inlet Creek. We are 9,500 feet above sea level here. There are 780 feet and approximately 2 miles left to hike. The next destination is Lone Pine Lake. Hike along the south side of the lake, and then cross a nice series of bridges. The first two have waterfalls. The trail continues to climb, and the surface is well maintained though very rocky. The last mile to the campsite is surprisingly easy. It travels along the creek and then eventually passes a hitching rail. Take a left onto the small trail that leads uphill to the Lake Verna Campsite: this is where you stop for the night. The campsite itself is only a small clearing in the forest with space for your tent and a separate cooking area. You may want to spend your time at the beautiful area below your campsite, the shore of Lake Verna. Have a good rest, and in the morning head back the way you came.

DIRECTIONS   From the Grand Lake Entrance Station, take US 34 west 1.6 miles and turn left into Grand Lake Village; stay on the left fork, West Portal Road, and travel 2.4 miles to the East Inlet Trailhead.

GPS TRAILHEAD COORDINATES
N40°14.247' W105°48.020'

29 East Shore Trailhead:
Shadow Mountain Lake and Ranger Meadows Balloon

SCENERY: ✿ ✿ ✿ ✿

DIFFICULTY: ✿ ✿

TRAIL CONDITION: ✿ ✿ ✿ ✿

DISTANCE: 6 miles, balloon

CHILDREN: ✿ ✿ ✿ ✿

SOLITUDE: ✿ ✿ ✿ ✿

HIKING TIME: 2.5 hours

OUTSTANDING FEATURES: Shadow Mountain Lake, Colorado River, creeks, meadows, lake scenery

---

THIS TRAIL IS A FAVORITE—the forested landscape along the lake and the tall grasses and wildflowers of Ranger Meadows are beautiful, and you'll enjoy the pristine paths and the fact that there aren't many hikers here. The trail crosses the boundary between Rocky Mountain National Park and the U.S. Forest Service; a difference between the two is not significant.

🚶🚶 Leave the parking lot and walk across the spillway of Shadow Mountain Dam. Shadow Mountain Lake is to the left, and to the right you'll see the water being let loose from the lake into the Colorado River, which then flows into Columbine Bay.

Reach the East Shore Trailhead and take a left onto the trail that enters Rocky Mountain National Park in 0.6 mile. The trail travels along a ridge on the east side of Shadow Mountain Lake. This section of the trail provides wonderful, scenic views out over the water. The trail surface is level, mostly packed dirt, and continues to follow the shore until it turns away from the lake at a gentle ascent and then continues into the forest.

The trail travels back around toward the lake. It's lush in some spots, marshy and muddy in others. Continue straight past the first intersection,

⊙ East Shore Trailhead: Shadow Mountain Lake and Ranger Meadows Balloon

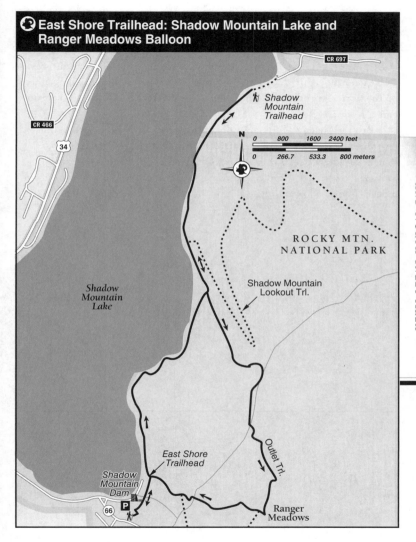

CR 697

🚶 *Shadow Mountain Trailhead*

N

| 0 | 800 | 1600 | 2400 feet |

| 0 | 266.7 | 533.3 | 800 meters |

CR 466

34

ROCKY MTN. NATIONAL PARK

Shadow Mountain Lake

Shadow Mountain Lookout Trl.

Outlet Trl.

East Shore Trailhead

Shadow Mountain Dam

66

P

Ranger Meadows

2 miles from the East Shore Trailhead. The trail rises up above the lake. Pass a sign that says, ENTERING ROCKY MOUNTAIN NATIONAL PARK, SHADOW MOUNTAIN LOOKOUT 4.8 MILES AND SHADOW MOUNTAIN DAM 2.8 MILES. The Shadow Mountain Lookout Trail is a strenuous trek to a unique, historic fire lookout. Continue to the Shadow Mountain Trailhead on the north side of the hike and turn around. Trace back the trail that you have already traveled.

Pass the Shadow Mountain Lookout sign again and head back to the next intersection, where hikers turn left onto Outlet Trail and head to Ranger Meadows. Cross over Ranger Creek, where the trail is overgrown with meadow grasses. Continue through the meadow, keeping an eye out for moose. The meadow and the trail skirt in and out of the edge of the forest.

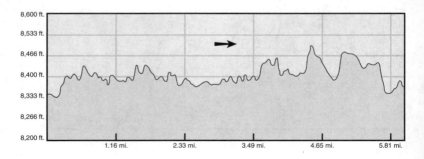

At the next trail intersection, turn right up the hill, following the directions to East Shore Trail and Shadow Mountain Dam. Cross over a marshy bog on one of the long, split-log double bridges and then come back out on the trail. The last intersection puts you back at the East Shore Trailhead. Travel along the Colorado River, climbing up the right side of the dam. Head left, back across the dam, and back to the parking lot.

DIRECTIONS   From the Grand Lake Entrance Station, take US 34 west past the Grand Lake Village for 2.8 miles to a left turn into Green Ridge Complex (CO 66). Travel 1 mile, and make a left turn into the campground. Drive up toward the lake, turn right into the next campground, and park at the Shadow Mountain Dam. Pay the U.S. Forest Service fee at Shadow Mountain Dam.

GPS TRAILHEAD COORDINATES
N40°12.219' W105°50.449'

30 Green Mountain Trailhead:
Tonahutu Creek Trail to Renegade Campsite to Flattop Mountain

---

SCENERY: ✩ ✩ ✩ ✩ ✩

DIFFICULTY: ✩ ✩ ✩ ✩

TRAIL CONDITION: ✩ ✩ ✩

CHILDREN: ✩

SOLITUDE: ✩ ✩ ✩ ✩

HIKING TIME: 13 hours out-and-back to Flattop Mountain (8 hours out-and-back to Renegade Campsite); 9 hours for thru-hike (Green Mountain Trailhead to Bear Lake Trailhead)

DISTANCE: 23.2 miles out-and-back to Flattop Mountain (14.6 miles out-and-back to Renegade Campsite); 16 miles thru-hike (Green Mountain Trailhead to Bear Lake Trailhead)

OUTSTANDING FEATURES: Meadows, forest, timberline, tundra, waterfall, creek

---

THIS IS A RARE HIKE that traverses the Continental Divide and takes hikers from the west side of Rocky Mountain National Park to the east side. Renegade is a good stopping point and an even better campsite. There are plenty of options in this hike; the first is to start at Green Mountain Trailhead, camp at Renegade, hike to Flattop Mountain, and then turn around. If you want to hike to Renegade, camp, and then turn around, that's great, too. A final option is to hike from Green Mountain Trailhead to Bear Lake Trailhead. This requires arranging a shuttle ride from either trailhead.

🚶🚶 From the parking lot, leave the trailhead and start on the 1.8-mile uphill trek to Big Meadow. The first part of the trail is wide, packed dirt, and very easy to navigate albeit quite steep. The trail then moderates for the remaining mile to Big Meadow. Cross a number of large wooden bridges and pass several meadows through the trees on the right. Each meadow is

Green Mountain Trailhead: Tonahutu Creek Trail to Renegade Campsite to Flattop Mountain

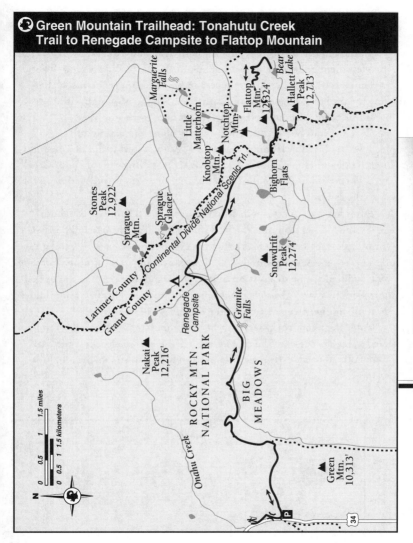

Marguerite Falls

Bear Lake

Hallett Peak 12,713'

Flattop Mtn. 12,324'

Little Matterhorn

Notchtop Mtn.

Knobtop Mtn.

Bighorn Flats

Stones Peak 12,922'

Sprague Mtn.

Sprague Glacier

Continental Divide National Scenic Trl.

Snowdrift Peak 12,274'

Larimer County

Grand County

Renegade Campsite

Granite Falls

Nakai Peak 12,216'

ROCKY MTN. NATIONAL PARK

BIG MEADOWS

Onahu Creek

Green Mtn. 10,313'

34

N

0   0.5   1   1.5 miles
0   0.5   1   1.5 kilometers

progressively bigger than the one before it. A short downhill brings hikers to the largest meadow, which lives up to its name: Big Meadow.

At the intersection of Green Mountain Trail and Tonahutu Creek Trail, take a left turn. Follow the trail along the north side of Big Meadow. There are remnants of an old cabin to the left and more cabin remnants farther along the trail to the right. Your destination, Flattop Mountain, is not visible at this point, although other high peaks have come into view.

Take the trail north and then curve east along the far end of Big Meadow. Big Meadow is about a mile long. At the intersection of Tonahutu Creek Trail and Onahu Creek Trail, bear right, staying on Tonahutu Creek Trail. Then head back into the trees, heading in an easterly direction all the way to the campsite.

After hiking a quarter mile into the trees, you'll come to Tonahutu Creek, which flows alongside the trail for a while. Pass Sunset and Sunrise Campsites on the left. There is a slight grade in the trail, and then it levels off. This is a pleasant walk in the woods with nothing of great note, and then you'll suddenly come to a section of steep rock and stairs. At the top of that short section, Lower Granite Falls Campsite is to the right. In a few minutes, you'll hit another steep section, as the hike grows more difficult.

After the steep, rocky section, the trail comes to Granite Falls, a two-tiered water cascade over the rocks. Take a break near the rocks at the base of the falls. Another extremely steep section brings hikers to Granite Falls

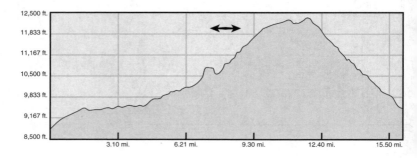

Haynach Campsite is one of many campsites along this trail. These sites are closer to the trail-head and not featured here, but llamas are permitted and always a fun option for packing it in.

Campsite on the left. Cross over the bridge and cross a large meadow that offers new views of the surrounding mountain peaks.

Tonahutu Creek's water thunders along the trail through here. Keep hiking through the trees on the rocky trail. Arrive at Tonahutu Meadows and Tonahutu Meadows Campsites on the east end of the meadow. Pass the intersection of the trail that goes downhill to the Tonahutu Stock Campsite. Be sure to go uphill to the left of this intersection.

Up to this point, the trail has been well trodden, probably because of the close campsites. But now the trail we are on is much smaller, and less frequently traveled. It is still steep, the creek tumbling along by our side. Cross the creek and pass the Haynach Campsite.

Hiking from west to east in Rocky Mountain National Park is a rare undertaking, but this overnight hike offers the option. Pictured here is Flattop Mountain, just behind Bear Lake, and a nice endpoint on this thru-hike after a stay at Renegade Campsite.

Some of the trees here are quite large for being right below timberline. There is a sharp left in the trail, and in 100 feet you will see the sign for Renegade Campsite on the left. A silver arrow a few hundred feet up the trail marks the campsite. Campers are supposed to camp within 15 feet of this arrow. Although the site sits on a slant, it's a little bit bigger and more open than the usual tent areas at backcountry sites. The trees are large but well spaced. There are views of the surrounding peaks through the trees. This will be our stop for the night. Paths lead off to the left to another possible campsite, although not within the 15 feet of the silver arrow. There are rocks and stumps around for sitting and setting up camp.

In the morning, go back down to the main trail and take a left turn. Continue up the hill. In a few minutes, you will be in the shadow of Sprague

Mountain, hiking toward an old rockslide. As we approach the front of the rockslide, the trail makes an abrupt curve to the right.

Pass the turnoff to Timberline Campsite, a group site, to the left. Cross a split-log bridge and come to a warning sign. This is a 3-D map of what is to come in the trail—basically a warning that you'll go through Bighorn Flats for several miles above treeline. There is severe weather with snow whiteouts, even in summer. Hikers can easily lose their way in the snow or the fog.

The trail takes a right and crosses debris at the base of the rockslide. Continue up; views from this point are tremendous, with snow-covered peaks across the valley to the right. The trail is extremely rough and rocky; continue to follow it through the car-size boulders and back into the tress. Even in late summer, water will be flowing down the trail during this section. Nakai Peak is over your right shoulder; it's also visible from the other direction down in Big Meadow. The traverse you are starting lasts about 0.75 mile. You'll cross numerous little creeks and streams. After a quarter mile you will exit the forest, although there are still a few stands of trees ahead. The trail goes up over the top of the ridge.

You will begin to see rock cairns at this point. You may notice a few points above you on the traverse where there are some little used switchbacks that are extremely steep and hard to follow. This is not the trail and not where we want to go. After a stand of trees, the trail climbs a little bit and continues across the tundra. Snow off to the right commands much of the view. A level mountain that you can see in front of us is not Flattop Mountain, just a false summit.

We continue to cross Bighorn Flats through open tundra for about 2 miles. Frequent cairns, often only 100 yards apart, guide hikers as we head to the northern shoulder of Bighorn Flats. Storm Peak comes into view over your left shoulder and Knobtop Mountain is the next landmark in front of us. The trail veers to the south for a half mile and back east toward Ptarmigan Point, the knobby protrusion in front of you.

From the trail you can see the Grand Valley. The grade here is extremely mild, and walking is very easy, even though we've been traveling above 12,000 feet for quite a while now. Keep heading straight up the top of Bighorn Flats. There are very few turns here but enough marmots to keep you entertained.

As you get below the rocky crag in front of us, the trail veers southwest, going a little bit to the right. Hikers suddenly have clear views of Grand Lake and Shadow Mountain Lake, both way, way down the mountain. The trail veers to the right side of Ptarmigan Point and goes back east again for half a mile to Flattop Mountain. From this side, Flattop Mountain is a terminus of Bighorn Flats; it's more rugged on the other side. Hallett Peak is directly in front of you and stands at 12,713 feet, making it now the nearest and most prominent landmark. That's where we head now.

You can see the trail straight ahead, and visibility is good for a long time. There is a very rugged view beyond that and rugged drop-offs coming into view on the left. Go around Ptarmigan Point, and the trail actually goes downhill before going back up to the top of Flattop Mountain. If the weather is good, go over to the viewpoint on the left just before Flattop Mountain. There are tremendous views looking down to three lakes that lie below.

This is not a good place to wander off the trail if visibility is bad. In Bighorn Flats it was fairly safe, but from here on, there are some tremendous drop-offs to the left. From the overlook it's back uphill at a mild grade. Pass the intersection with North Inlet Trail and continue straight up the hill. Next stop is the top of Flattop Mountain.

From here you can turn around and go back to Renegade Campsite for the night and then back to the Green Mountain Trailhead. Or you can head east down to the Bear Lake Trailhead.

DIRECTIONS   From the Grand Lake Entrance Station, take US 34 east 2.8 miles to the Green Mountain Trailhead. Turn right into the parking lot.

GPS TRAILHEAD COORDINATES
N40°18.305' W105°50.440'

31 Onahu Creek Trailhead:
Onahu Creek Trail and Green Mountain Trail Loop

SCENERY: ✿ ✿ ✿ ✿

DIFFICULTY: ✿ ✿ ✿

TRAIL CONDITION: ✿ ✿ ✿ ✿

DISTANCE: 7.6 miles, loop

CHILDREN: ✿ ✿ ✿

SOLITUDE: ✿ ✿ ✿ ✿

HIKING TIME: 4 hours

OUTSTANDING FEATURES: Loop hike, Big Meadow, Onahu Creek, homesteader remnants, lodgepole-pine forest, aspen trees, a lot of shade

---

AT LAST, A LONG LOOP HIKE in Rocky Mountain National Park. Believe me, loop day hikes are hard to come by in the park. This hike is a quiet walk in the woods—the only sound you'll hear is the slightly spooky creaking of fallen lodgepole pines. By combining Onahu Creek, Tonahutu, and Green Mountain Trails, you form a circle through some amazing scenery. This is a long, uncrowded walk with a variety of creeks, streams, cascades, aspen trees, and more. Be sure to bring along a buddy and plenty of supplies.

🥾   Leave the Onahu Creek Trailhead, taking a left turn onto the trail. It's a 6.9-mile trek to the Green Mountain Trailhead, and then another 0.7 mile to make it back to this trailhead.

The first destination to set your sights on is the Onahu Bridge, which is 3 miles from the trailhead.

The trail travels along the edge of Trail Ridge Road at first; it's a level, dirt singletrack, and in the summer it's lined with grasses and wildflowers. The trail begins to turn away from the road and travels at a slight ascent through a mix of meadow and forest.

As you travel deeper into the forest, the trees become dense and ferns cover the moist ground. There are many fallen trees here, and they creak when a breeze rolls in. It's almost like the sound of an old door being opened in a haunted house. You'll find yourself looking over your shoulder more than once.

Pass through a few gentle switchbacks and continue through a small aspen grove. The trail then makes a moderate descent as it passes through aspens that have been scratched and scarred by animals.

Continue to meander up and down the roller-coaster trail. So far, the trail has been quite mossy, and when we hiked in midsummer, there were a lot of bugs—mostly mosquitoes—and trees full of mossy lichen.

Begin another small descent while approaching a small stream. Cross the water on a split-log bridge and then travel up again to where the trail levels out and follows a hillside in a long, deep switchback. The trail levels out again and enters the dense forest. Begin another climb along a hillside; you'll hear and then see a cascading waterfall on your left.

The next waypoint is Onahu Creek, which we've been traveling along for a while now. Cross over it on a stout bridge and begin to travel upward again. Come back around toward the creek and cross another bridge, spanning a stream that feeds into Onahu Creek.

The trail continues to travel uphill with the sound of Onahu Creek on the right. It then levels out and travels along a flat, forested area. There are many rocks and trees in the path. Pass the signs that direct backpackers to backcountry campsites: Onahu Creek, Upper Onahu, and Onahu Bridge.

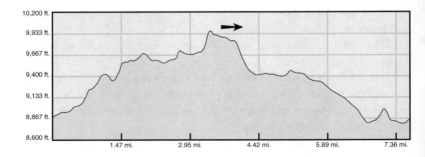

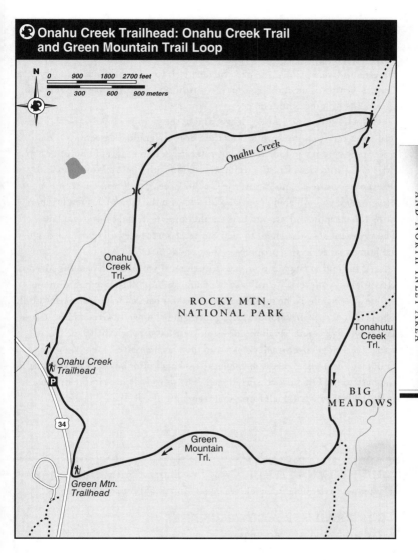

Onahu Creek Trailhead: Onahu Creek Trail and Green Mountain Trail Loop

N

0   900   1800   2700 feet
0   300   600   900 meters

Onahu Creek

Onahu Creek Trl.

ROCKY MTN. NATIONAL PARK

Onahu Creek Trailhead

P

34

Green Mountain Trl.

Green Mtn. Trailhead

Tonahutu Creek Trl.

BIG MEADOWS

On the right, a large meadow opens up through the trees. The trail is still level and has gotten softer and sandier. The trail starts to go uphill again and continues alongside Onahu Creek on the right. Take the Onahu Bridge over the Onahu Creek. Continue past the next sign toward the Tonahutu Creek Trail, 1.5 miles. The climb resumes, continuing uphill and passing through a rockslide of large boulders.

The trail travels up a steep ledge, and to the right is a big drop-off. The trail levels out for a short while, and then begins a gradual descent; it is narrower now, and if you look to the left you can see a tree-covered mountain ridge come into view. Pass the trail intersection with Flattop Mountain and Bear Lake. You're 4.5 miles past the Onahu Creek Trailhead. Continue straight, and you will come upon Big Meadow on the left. Walk a few minutes along the meadow and you will pass an old homestead and cabin remnants. Their presence is a testament to Sam Stone's taste for views. He was the original homesteader on this property in the early 1900s.

At the end of Big Meadow, pass a hitch rack; you also will pass Big Meadow Campsite on your left. We will take the main trail uphill to Green Mountain trailhead, 1.8 miles. The uphill is short, and you have a long pleasant downhill. The path is wide, fairly smooth, and gently graded down to Green Mountain Trailhead. Pass several small meadows on your left through the trees. Cross a series of bridges over small creeks, and then arrive at the Green Mountain Trailhead. From here, cross through the parking lot to the trail that will take you back to the Onahu Creek Trailhead. The short walk back to the original trailhead is through a small forest that travels alongside Trail Ridge Road.

DIRECTIONS   From the Grand Lake Entrance Station, take US 34 east 3.3 miles to the Onahu Creek Trailhead. Turn right into the parking lot.

GPS TRAILHEAD COORDINATES
N40°18.338' W105°50.363'

APPENDIX A:
Camping Equipment Checklist

SUMMER BACKPACKING GEAR CHECKLIST

- Backpack
- Tent and rainfly
- Sleeping bag and sleeping pad or mattress
- Water filter or purification tablets
- Water bottles
- Flashlight *(with new batteries)*
- Extra batteries
- Candle lantern *(optional)*
- Trowel or small shovel for digging cat holes
- Pocketknife
- Bear canister
- 50 feet of rope and nylon cord
- Topographical map and GPS unit
- Toilet paper and plastic bags for packing it out
- Biodegradable hand soap
- Toothbrush and toothpaste
- Small towel
- Bandannas
- Whistle
- Stuff sacks
- Sewing kit
- Food *(include extra for emergencies)*
- Cooking pots/pans *(nesting)*
- Eating utensils *(cup, bowl, plate, knife, fork, spoon)*

- Cleaning supplies *(biodegradable detergent and container, sponge, scouring pad)*
- Waterproof matches in waterproof container
- Stove and fuel
- Collapsible bucket or water bag
- Hat
- Poncho or rain gear
- Boots
- Boot socks
- Sock liners
- Long pants
- Shorts
- Light shirt or T-shirt
- Warm shirt
- Jacket or outerwear *(layer clothing)*
- Other clothing depending on conditions and altitude
- Appropriate undergarments

FIRST-AID KIT

- Pain reliever
- Band-Aids
- First-aid cream
- Gauze pads
- Insect repellent
- Moleskin
- UV sunblock, lip balm
- Personal medications
- Adhesive tape

APPENDIX B: *Rocky Mountain National Park Backcountry Camping Guide*

How to Get Your Permit

YOU MUST HAVE A PERMIT to camp overnight in Rocky Mountain National Park's backcountry. You can pick one up at the Headquarters Backcountry Office (beside the Beaver Meadows Visitor Center on CO 36 west of Estes Park) or at the Kawuneeche Visitor Center (CO 34, north of Grand Lake on the west side of Rocky Mountain National Park).

To minimize impacts on the park's resources, a limited number of permits are issued. You can reserve a summer permit by phone, mail, or in person between March 1 and May 15, and by mail or in person between May 16 and September 30. Reservations for winter, spring, and fall permits can be made by phone, mail, or in person from Jan. 1–May 15 and Oct. 1–Dec. 31; and by mail or in person May 16–Sept. 30.

CONTACT INFORMATION:

Rocky Mountain National Park
Backcountry Office
1000 West Hwy. 36
Estes Park, CO 80517
970-586-1242; 970-586-1319 (TDD)
go.nps.gov/rockybackcountry

FOR ALL RESERVATIONS:

1. Include your name, address, zip code, and telephone number.
2. List an itinerary with dates corresponding to campsites where you plan to stay.
3. Specify the number of people that will be in your party. (Limit of seven per party for individual campsites. Limit of 8 to 12 per party for group campsites.)

4. There is a $26 wilderness administrative fee for each reservation (not each night) from May 1–October 31 (non-refundable and non-exchangeable). You will receive a confirmation letter after your reservation has been processed. The wilderness administrative fee must be paid at **pay.gov** within 24 hours of receiving the confirmation letter, or your reservation will be canceled. There is no fee in winter.

During the winter and early spring, when the backcountry is not as frequently used, you may self-register at the Wild Basin Entrance, Trailhead, Longs Peak Ranger Station, Dunraven Trailhead, and Fall River and Beaver Meadows entrance stations.

During the busy summer months, if you have a permit reservation, you must pick up the permit by 10 a.m. on the first day of your planned backcountry stay; otherwise, the permit will be canceled in its entirety and given to other backpackers. If you know you will not be using your permit, please cancel your reservation as soon as possible.

How to Use the Permit

YOUR PERMIT IS A CONTRACT with the National Park Service—you're agreeing to take care of the wilderness and treat the backcountry with respect.

You will see backcountry regulations on the back of each permit. Read, understand, sign, and obey them. The backcountry use permit must be easily accessible and with you at all times. A tent tag must be displayed on the outside of your pack while hiking to your campsite and on your tent at the campsite. The permit indicates the number of people in your party and specifies a campsite for each night you are in the backcountry. You must stick with your planned itinerary so that campsites do not become overcrowded and overused.

In addition to a permit, you will receive a dash tag, to be placed on the dashboard of your vehicle. Since overnight parking is only allowed with a backcountry permit, failure to properly display a dash tag may result in a citation and/or a towing fee.

Permit Parameters

INDIVIDUAL PARTIES consist of one to seven people. Each party is assigned one campsite.

Each camping area has one to six sites. We recommend you travel in small parties because fewer people per site leaves less impact on the park's fragile resources.

Groups consist of 8 to 12 people. They must camp at special group sites. Due to impacts caused by group interaction in and between sites (site spread, social trails, and so on), groups of more than seven persons may not camp in neighboring individual sites, and instead must use group sites or split up and camp at least 1 mile apart.

Between June and September, campers may stay in the backcountry for a maximum of seven nights, with no more than three consecutive nights in one camp area. Between October and May, campers may stay in the backcountry for a maximum of 14 nights. So, campers can stay in the backcountry for a total of 21 nights each year.

Setting Out on Your Trip

ALWAYS TELL SOMEONE at home your trip itinerary and when you will return. Allow plenty of time for your trip. Consider the distance you plan to travel, the elevation of the trailhead and your destination, the amount of weight you are carrying, your physical condition, current and forecasted weather, and the hours of daylight remaining.

- Read the trailhead bulletin board.
- Plan to be below treeline during the afternoon when thunderstorms and lightning most often occur.
- Pets, weapons, and vehicles (including mountain bikes) are not allowed in the backcountry.
- Don't forget insect repellent to fend off mosquitoes. Check frequently for ticks.

- Be considerate of others and the resources.
- Set a pace that is comfortable for all members of your party.
- Stay on the trail and hike single file. Resist the temptation to walk off the trail when it is muddy. Mud will flake off your boots much sooner than trampled plants will grow back.
- Never shortcut switchbacks.
- Pick up litter you find along the way.
- Horses and llamas have the right-of-way. Step off the trail on the downhill side and stand quietly until the stock passes.
- Never leave food unattended. Properly store your food.
- Never feed animals.
- When you pause to take a break, sit on rocks or clearings rather than on vegetation.
- Do not disturb any flowers or plants.

Check upcoming weather before departing. Remember, conditions can change quickly!

Sanitation

THERE ARE PIT TOILETS at many backcountry campsites. When a pit toilet is not available, do the following:

- Urinate in rocky places that won't be damaged by animals who dig for the salts and minerals found in urine.
- Dig a hole 6 inches (15 centimeters) deep for solid waste using a small trowel, or pack out waste and paper.
- Be sure that you defecate at least 70 adult steps (200 feet/60 meters) from water or trails.
- Do not bury sanitary napkins or tampons. Dispose of them in an airtight container, and pack them out.
- Wash hands with biodegradable soap. Giardia and other diseases are frequently spread by unsanitary habits.

Please Respect the Fragile Tundra

ALPINE-TUNDRA VEGETATION IS HARDY. These plants survive extreme cold, strong winds, intense ultraviolet radiation, and very low humidity. Yet, as tough as these plants are, they cannot withstand repeated trampling. It takes 100 years for many alpine-tundra plants to grow an inch.

You may walk on the alpine tundra only in places where there are no maintained trails, or in undeveloped areas, but do not walk in single file. Spread out, so that your footprints are not concentrated on a small area, and rock-hop instead of stepping on vegetation.

At Camp

WHEN YOU ARRIVE AT YOUR DESTINATION, you will see trail signs that show where to find campsites. Pitch your tent in designated areas. Don't pitch your tent on undisturbed vegetation, and never dig or trench around a tent.

There are no grizzly bears in Rocky Mountain National Park, but black bears do live here. Help park rangers keep bears and other animals (including mice, marmots, martens, porcupines, and deer) from becoming a problem by taking precautions with your food and garbage.

■ A portable food-storage container is perhaps the best method to secure your food and scented items.

■ Another option is to hang your food from a tree. The counterbalance technique is recommended. Suspend your food at least 10 feet (about 3 meters) above the ground and 4 horizontal feet (about 1.2 meters) from the tree trunk. It takes at least 50 feet of rope and two stuff sacks to successfully execute this technique. Not all camp areas have trees that are appropriate for hanging items. Inquire at the backcountry office.

■ Keep a clean camp.

■ Seal uneaten food scraps and all garbage in airtight containers or storage bags, and carry all garbage out of the backcountry.

- Refrain from packing greasy, smelly foods into the backcountry.
- Keep all scented items out of your tent including soap, deodorant, and toothpaste. Store them with your food.
- *Beware:* Deer, bighorn sheep, porcupines, and other animals are attracted to sweat and urine. These animals can destroy campsites, clothes, boots, and camping gear in search of salt. Hang your gear and use proper backcountry sanitation.

Preparing Meals at Camp

COOK MEALS WITH A PORTABLE STOVE. Do not plan to build a fire. Fires are comforting and aesthetically pleasing, but they cause considerable impact on the backcountry. Wood is better used for habitat for wild creatures than as fuel for campers whose lives do not depend upon forest resources. Campfires have potential to get out of control if not well tended. For these reasons, fires are only allowed in a few designated campsites that have metal fire rings. Never take food in the sleeping area. Separate where you eat from where you sleep.

Drinking Water

ALWAYS PURIFY THE DRINKING WATER you get in the backcountry with one of the following methods:
- Filter water with a portable purification system that eliminates giardia.
- Boil water for 10 minutes.
- Use water-purifying tablets or drops that eliminate giardia.

Wash Water

CARRY WATER AT LEAST 70 adult steps (200 feet/60 meters) from a lake or stream to wash yourself or your dishes. Use biodegradable soap. When disposing of wash water, first filter out all food scraps with a small screen.

Pack the food scraps into an airtight container to be carried out later. Then toss out the wash water by throwing it over a wide area.

- Never wash directly in a lake or stream.
- Do not scatter food scraps in the water or on the ground.
- Do not throw food into pit toilets.
- Pack out all food scraps, trash, and uneaten food.

Leaving the Backcountry

IF YOU END A TRIP EARLY, notify a ranger to cancel the permit, so other backpackers may take your place. Please report all unusual wildlife sightings, trail conditions, or incidents to a ranger. Pack out all your garbage and that of others less considerate. If you see any violations of rules and regulations, please report them to a ranger as soon as possible. You can find showers and laundry facilities in Estes Park and in Grand Lake.

Fishing

TO FISH IN ROCKY MOUNTAIN NATIONAL PARK you must have a Colorado state fishing license. You may purchase licenses at local sporting-goods stores. Check out fishing regulations at Rocky Mountain National Park visitor centers. Ask for the fishing brochure.

Packing with Wheelchairs: *Sprague Lake Camp*

THERE IS A SPECIAL WHEELCHAIR-ACCESSIBLE backcountry campsite near Sprague Lake, a half mile from the trailhead. The camp accommodates up to 12 campers, including up to five wheelchairs. To make reservations, please use the same permit process described on pages 181–182.

Packing with Horses or Llamas

There are special stock campsites and rules for overnight camping with stock. Some trails are closed to stock use. Call 970-586-1206 or 970-586-1242 for more information. Ask for the "Horse and Pack Animals" brochure.

Backcountry Camping Rules and Regulations

As we mentioned above, a permit is required for all overnight backcountry use and must be displayed on the outside of your pack while you hike to your campsite and also on your tent at the site.

- The permit is valid only for the dates and camp areas listed.
- A displayed dash tag is required for overnight parking.
- Camp must be established on designated tent pads where provided, or within 15 feet of the metal arrowhead that marks the designated site.
- Use pit toilets where provided; otherwise, dig a 6-inch-deep cat hole at least 200 feet (70 adult steps) from water, trails, and campsites.

General Regulations

In order to protect park resources and minimize impacts, the following are prohibited everywhere in the backcountry:

- Pets, weapons, and vehicles (including bicycles)
- Fires (except at specific sites with metal fire rings)
- Hunting, feeding, approaching, or disturbing wildlife
- Removing or disturbing natural features
- Trenching around tents and camps
- Shortcutting between trail switchbacks
- Littering or leaving trash in sites or pit toilets
- Washing dishes or bathing within 200 feet (70 adult steps) of water.

Special Regulations

DESIGNATED SITES:

- Camp must be established within 15 feet of the metal arrowhead and post that mark the site.

- Use stoves only. Fires prohibited, unless staying in a *wood fire site* with visible metal fire ring (using dead and down wood only).

- Party size is limited to 7 at individual sites and 12 at group sites.

- Due to excessive impact, groups of more than seven persons must use group sites or split up and camp at least 1 mile apart.

- If the designated site has more than 4 inches of snow, follow the winter regulations detailed in a pamphlet available at the backcountry office or online.

RMNP BACKCOUNTRY CAMPING GUIDE

APPENDIX B:

APPENDIX C: *Contact Information*

National Park Service: Rocky Mountain National Park

Beaver Meadows Visitor Center
1000 US 36
Estes Park, CO 80517

Kawuneeche Visitor Center
16018 US 34
Grand Lake, CO 80447

Information office: 970-586-1206
Recorded message: 970-586-1222
Trail Ridge Road Status *(recorded message on the current road status)*: 970-586-1222
Backcountry information: 970-586-1242
Recorded information and road and weather conditions: 970-586-1333
nps.gov/romo
Facebook, Twitter, Instagram, Flickr, YouTube

Colorado Department of Transportation Road Conditions
877-315-7623 or **cotrip.org**

Estes Park Visitor Center
800-443-7837 or 970-577-9900 or **visitestespark.com**

Grand Lake Chamber of Commerce
800-531-1019

Grand Lake Chamber of Commerce Visitor Center
P.O. Box 57
Grand Lake, CO 80447
970-627-3402 or **grandlakechamber.com**

Grand Lake Metro Recreation District
P.O. Box 590
Grand Lake, CO 80447
970-627-8328 or **grandlakerecreation.com**

Larimer County Parks and Open Lands Department

1800 South County Rd. 31
Loveland, CO 80537
970-679-4570 or **larimer.org/parks**

Rocky Mountain Nature Association

1895 Fall River Rd.
Estes Park, CO 80517
800-748-7002 or 970-586-3262 or **rmconservancy.org**

U.S. FOREST SERVICE:
Arapaho and Roosevelt National Forests, Pawnee National Grassland

THE ARAPAHO AND ROOSEVELT NATIONAL FORESTS surround Rocky Mountain National Park. For further information, contact the Arapaho and Roosevelt National Forest Fort Collins Ranger Station at 970-295-6700; the Boulder Ranger Station at 303-541-2500; the Granby Ranger Station at 970-887-4100; and the Arapaho National Recreation Area (Lake Granby area) at 970-887-4100.

Roosevelt National Forest information:

Estes-Poudre Ranger District Office

161 Second St.
P.O. Box 2747
Estes Park, CO 80517 or 970-586-3440

Boulder Ranger District

2140 Yarmouth Ave.
Boulder, CO 80301
303-541-2500 or **www.fs.usda.gov**

Canyon Lakes Ranger District

2150 Centre Ave., Building E
Fort Collins, CO 80526
970-295-6700 or **www.fs.usda.gov**

Pawnee National Grassland

660 O St.
Greeley, CO 80631
970-346-5000 or **www.fs.usda.gov**

Sulphur Ranger District

9 Ten Mile Dr., P.O. Box 10
Granby, CO 80446
970-887-4100

Colorado Travel and Tourism

800-265-6723 or **colorado.com**

APPENDIX D: *Online Map Resources*

■ Brunton **brunton.com**

■ DeLorme **delorme.com**

■ EMS **ems.com**

■ Garmin **garmin.com**

■ Magellan **magellangps.com**

■ Mapquest **mapquest.com**

■ Maptech, Inc. **maptech.com**

■ Microsoft Mapblast **mapblast.com**

■ National Geographic MapMachine **nationalgeographic.com/mapmachine**

■ National Geographic Maps **nationalgeographic.com/maps**

■ Offroute **offroute.com**

■ REI **rei.com**

■ Suunto **suunto.com**

■ TopoZone **topozone.com**

■ U.S. Forest Service **www.fs.fed.us**

Maps by phone:

303-275-5350; 303-275-5367 (hearing-impaired)
Maps available at all local agency offices

Maps by mail:

Visitor Map Sales
P.O. Box 25127
Lakewood, CO 80225

■ U.S. Geological Survey **usgs.gov**

■ USGS Map Store **store.usgs.gov**

APPENDIX E: *Websites*

- Access Fund **accessfund.org**
- Active.com **active.com**
- American Hiking Society **americanhiking.org**
- American Trails **americantrails.org**
- America Walks **americawalks.org**
- Climb the Rockies **climbtherockies.com**
- Colorado Fourteeners Initiative **14ers.org**
- Colorado Mountain Club **cmc.org**
- Colorado Trail Foundation **coloradotrail.org**
- Continental Divide Trail Coalition **continentaldividetrail.org**
- Fourteeners.org **fourteeners.org**
- Geocache Resources **geocaching.com**
- Happy Hikers Club **happyhikersclub.org**
- Hiking and Backpacking **hikingandbackpacking.org/coloradoclubs**
- Hiking in Colorado **hikingincolorado.org**
- Letterboxing **letterboxing.org**
- Mountain Peaks **mountainpeaks.net**
- Road Runner Club of America **rrca.org**
- Rocky Mountain Nature Association **rmna.org**
- Running Network **runningnetwork.com**
- Run Walk Jog **runwalkjog.com**
- Sierra Club **sierraclub.org/rocky-mountain-chapter**
- Trails.com **trails.com**
- Volunteers for Outdoor Colorado **voc.org**

APPENDIX F: *Bibliography*

Dannen, Kent, and Donna Dannen. *Best Easy Day Hikes: Rocky Mountain National Park.* Best Easy Day Hikes Ser. Guilford, CT: Falcon–Globe Pequot, 2002.

Dannen, Kent, and Donna Dannen. *Hiking Rocky Mountain National Park: Including Indian Peaks Wilderness.* 9th ed. Falcon Guides Hiking. Guilford, CT: Falcon–Globe Pequot, 2002.

Donahue, Mike. *The Longs Peak Experience and Trail Guide.* Indiana Camp Supply, 1992.

Dziezynski, James. *Best Summit Hikes in Colorado.* 2nd ed. Berkeley: Wilderness Press, 2012.

Fogelberg, Ben, and Steve Grinstead. *Walking into Colorado's Past:50 Front Range History Hikes.* Englewood, CO: Westcliffe Publishers, 2006.

Foster, Lisa. *Rocky Mountain National Park: The Complete Hiking Guide.* Rev. ed.Renaissance Mountaineering, 2013.

Hailman, Jack, and Elizabeth Hailman. *Hiking Circuits in Rocky Mountain National Park.* Boulder: UP of Colorado, 2003.

Malitz, Jerome. *Rocky Mountain National Park: Dayhiker's Guide.* Rev. ed. Boulder: Johnson, 2008.

Rusk, Dave, and Hal Rusk. *Rocky Mountain Day Hikes: Featuring 24 Hikes in RMNP.* 2nd ed. Estes Park, CO: Barefoot, 1999.

Salcedo, Tracy. *12 Short Hikes: Rocky Mountain National Park Estes Park.* 12 Short Hikes Ser. Guilford, CT: Falcon–Globe Pequot, 1997.

Salcedo, Tracy. *12 Short Hikes: Rocky Mountain National Park Grand Lake.* 12 Short Hikes Ser. Chockstone Press, 1997.

For additional Rocky Mountain National Park books, visit the Rocky Mountain Nature Association's website, **rmna.org.**

INDEX

INDEX

ABOUT THE AUTHOR

KIM LIPKER IS A NATIVE OF COLORADO and is the author of three other guidebooks and their updates for Menasha Ridge Press: *60 Hikes within 60 Miles: Denver and Boulder,* first and second editions; *Best Tent Camping: Colorado,* fourth and fifth editions (with Johnny Molloy); and *Smart and Savvy Hiking for Women*; along with *The Unofficial Guide to Bed & Breakfasts and Country Inns in the Rockies,* published by Hungry Minds.

She also writes a regular parenting column and other features for *Rocky Mountain Parent* magazine, and she contributes features, ratings, and reviews for Orbitz.com and Away.com, covering parks, active sports, and outdoor adventures in the Rocky Mountains and Hawaii.

Considered an expert on the Rocky Mountains by her guidebook peers, Kim has been at the writing thing for a while, having had her first news article published at age 12 and later earning a journalism degree from the University of Missouri–Columbia. Kim works for Poudre School District and lives in Fort Collins with her three children.

The Lipker Family hanging out in their beautiful, sunny hometown of Fort Collins, Colorado